LEMURIA

The Lost Continent of the Pacific

WISHAR S. CERVÉ

CONTENTS

Introduction	vii
The First Races of Man in America	1
Fascinating Incidents of the Past	13
Mysterious Forces of the Universe	25
The Land and the Living	37
The Mental and Psychic Development of the Lemurians	47
The Spirituality of the Lemurians	58
The Community Life of the Lemurians	64
Remarkable Achievements of the Lemurians	72
The Colonies and Descendants of the Lemurians	81
Mysterious California	95
Present Day Mystic Lemurians in California	108
Appendix I	123

*In appreciation of the first researches
into the history of the lost continents of
Atlantis and Lemuria
made by that brilliant
mind and soul,
Sir Francis Bacon
this book is dedicated to his memory
and everlasting greatness of character.
The Author*

INTRODUCTION

I wish to anticipate many comments that will be made regarding this book by those who may have expected to find within its covers a scientific treatise on the subject. I have not attempted to make this book a treatise on the subjects of anthropology or anthropometry, nor in the fields of archaeological and geological research. Nor will meteorologists, astronomers, cosmologists or others find herein a ponderous encyclopedia of technical information.

With the same enormous mass of facts which I have had at my disposal, and with the same artists and other assistants ready and qualified to prepare matter in a technical form for me, such a book as some may anticipate could have been prepared and offered to the public, or to that limited portion of the public, desiring its knowledge in a technical form. But my purpose was to comply with the desires of the publishers in preparing and presenting an easily readable, enjoyable, and fascinating account of the lost Continent of Lemuria, with all of its past history, effects upon the races of man, and ancient, human incidents of life.

After all, it is a fact that all of us enjoy a relaxation from preachments and ponderous academic dissertations no matter how deeply we may be concerned with specialized scientific subjects. The very men who claim to cast aside a book that deals lightly with an historical, learned, or scientific subject are found in their times of relaxation completely lost and absorbed in the fascinating and alluring stories of the popular magazines and Sunday newspapers; and I do not hesitate to say that I have found among my scientific acquaintances many who have admittedly discovered their first dues to attractive subjects of research through the reading of the semi-scientific articles prepared for lay reading in the popular publications.

Scientific research and investigation may be substantial food to the scientific mind, but a readable story, brilliantly coloring the human interest side of the facts revealed by science, never falls to become food to the emotional, human, side of our natures.

The facts contained in this volume are arranged and presented in the same manner that the facts of life are presented to you dally. The serious points are mingled with those that are amusing or lightly interesting, instructive, or perhaps practical. The beam of the spotlight of interest is centered more upon the human interest features of the story than upon the ponderous technicalities of scientific erudition. The people, the characters, the scenes in the backgrounds, the facts and figures themselves, are all brought out of their laboratory niches and heavily draped positions, and paraded upon the stage of life before us to the accompaniment of lively music with the bright lights playing upon them while we, the readers in the audience, watch this age old play of life go on and on.

The story in this volume is a play of life that started over two hundred thousand years ago with a vague and indefinite prologue, and continuing through many astonishing, surprising, interesting, acts up to the present time. The play is still going on, for the descendants of Lemuria are still in our midst, and we are dally contacting the effects produced by these people who attained a high degree of civilization and established many principles of life which are still fixed in their purpose and practice.

After my task was started and I had overcome the hesitancy I had in writing lightly and freely in a non-technical manner of matters that might have been dealt with more deeply, I began to enjoy the work. I found the continents of which I was writing becoming alive, instead of dead, specimens painted on old yellow maps. The people themselves looked at me, talked to me, and told me their stories, and I found myself entering into their communities and observing the transitions in nature, the changes in all forms of life, and the evolution of the races of man. Then it was I discovered why the facts of the story of the lost continent of Lemuria had never reached a universal understanding among the lay-minds of the public. Only the geologists, archaeologists, profound historians and those who delve into the anthropology of man have found any interest in the history of Lemuria, and what they found they tabulated in such a dry and uninteresting manner and preserved as such sacred personal assets of their own achievements in research, that few knew what had actually been discovered.

I hope, therefore, that this book will make the subject more popular and arouse further interest in the investigation of the hundreds of available sources of information still untouched by those who have spent their lifetime seeking for positive facts.

With this hope and with the further desire that what I have written may contribute to a better understanding of the development of the human individual in all of his physical, mental, spiritual, and so-called psychic qualities, I offer this work.

W.S.C
July 7, 1931.

THE FIRST RACES OF MAN IN AMERICA

One of the most interesting problems in the study of world civilization is the origin of the first races of men in America. It has been commonly believed, as a popular idea, that the cradle of civilization was in Mesopotamia and there is a very general belief that the first races of man could be traced to some Oriental country. In fact, the so-called *Garden of Eden* has always been considered as a mythical description of an Oriental location.

A few years ago some scientists advanced the idea that the valley of the Ohio River might have been the real Garden of Eden, inasmuch as discoveries there tended to indicate that the mound builders and the cave dwellers may have descended from the first races of man to people the earth, and various relies unearthed in that valley seemed to be older than anything that had been found up to the period of their discovery. Since then further discoveries have changed the idea somewhat. While it is generally admitted that there is ample evidence to prove that the Ohio Valley did shelter and protect some races of man antedating the history of man in many other parts of the world, there are now many evidences to indicate that the Pacific Coast of the United States is unquestionably the only existing location of the earliest races of men who had reached a civilized state of development.

Many and various fantastic theories have been given to account for the presence of the aboriginal Americans. The history of the origin of the American Indian is a wonderful study and is a subject which may never be completely cleared of its mysteries.

The fact that the American Indians were divided into many tribes widely separated in their locations and widely differing in their language and yet appearing very much alike and having many customs and habits in common, permit of many forms of speculation as to their origin. The things which have been found to be common with most of the American Indian tribes afford a foundation for the theory that all of them were descendants of one race, while the many differences in their habits and customs and in their language afford a foundation for the theory that they were in no way related and that those in the western part of North America may have descended from other races that came from the West, while those in the eastern part of the continent were descendants of Eastern tribes or races who had made early contact with this continent.

In studying the problem we have many reliable scientific principles as guides and much data of an accumulative nature that constitutes a fairly dependable index. In studying the history of men we must bear in mind that there are certain characteristics which are common to all races and that slight variation may not always indicate distinct races but rather the effect of environment upon countenances, nature, and habits of man.

Certainly, we are face to face with one of the two possible explanations for the existence of the many races of man. Either all the races of man throughout the world had one common origin, in one cradle, in one location, and from this one point moved in all directions to cover the face of the earth, or man had his origin in many places throughout the world practically simultaneously. The question therefore is whether all mankind had one common origin and became differentiated in races and characteristics through evolution affected by environment as man moved to various parts of the world, or whether human beings evolved or were created in hundreds of widely scattered localities at the same time with distinct characteristics, natures, and habits in accordance with the purpose of creation and the environment in which the creation occurred.

Environment and the consequential effects of it will change the nature, appearance, habits, and customs of any race and it is perfectly possible for all of the races of man to have had one common origin and to have been identical in countenance, customs, and habits until the members of this one original race became scattered in various parts of the world and developed future generations having such modifications as the effect of environment would produce.

We know that men who live where there is an abundance of bright light such as in the northern or Southern polar regions or in countries having wide areas of snow for many months of the year, or where there is a great amount of white sand reflecting the brilliant sunlight, acquire squinting eyes or eyes which become slightly oblique, and from the squinting and continuous attempt to keep the eyes partly closed against the glaring light the cheek bones have a tendency to be raised or the muscles of the face are raised to appear like high cheek bones. On the other hand, those who live in the mountains or mountainous regions and must climb a great deal and struggle much in moving from place to place, soon develop strong legs, deep chests and powerfully developed muscles in the back, and these characteristics are transmitted from generation to generation until we have a different type of man from those living where there is snow or desert lands.

Likewise, the races of men who live along rivers or the borders of Oceans and have developed means of moving rafts or logs or other floating things for conveyances, using the arms as a motive power rather than the legs, soon develop broad chests and powerful shoulders with great muscular arms and under-developed legs.

Just these few points will indicate to you how physical characteristics may be developed in successive generations until an almost distinct race of man may be evolved through the effects of environment. If we add to these effects the additional ones of deeply tanned complexion in the warmer or brilliantly lighted climates or where there is a great deal of sunlight as in the north and south polar regions, and fairer complexions in the mountains or shaded valley sections of the temperate zones, and the effect upon the height and physical development generally resulting from warm or cold climates, accompanied by the effect upon the thickness, color and growth of the hair on the body, we will see that many greatly modified and diversified forms of the human body will evolve under the effects of environment.

We must not forget, either, the effect of food, water, and personal habits. The mental development of a race, adding to it the character of the soul within, also has an extremely important effect upon the outer appearance of man. It is generally conceded that the more intelligent races of man developed in those countries where the climate was extremely mild or cold while the less intelligent races developed in those countries where there was extreme heat. Analyzing this we find a very logical reason for this law. In the colder countries where there is much snow and ice man was forced to invent and reason out ways and means of clothing himself and protecting himself against the cold and the winds and he had to invent homes and shelter, and devise ways and means of warming them. H e had to devise ways and means of securing food and preserving it. All this taxed his imagination, challenged his mental ability, and made him more industrious and a deeper thinker. Those who lived in the very mild and warmer climates found an abundance of food the year around, required little or no clothing, no specially constructed homes or huts of any kind, and because of the heat and the enervating effects of the climate he became sluggish in his thinking and in his physical actions.

There are some modifications to the above and there are some indications of races that reached a high degree of culture in tropical climates, but most of these modifications are explained by the fact that those parts of the world that are now tropical may not have always been so tropical and those places which are now so completely covered with snow may have been more temperate in climate; and again many of the races of man that attained high civilization in tropical lands were descendants of tribes that came to such countries from more temperate or colder zones.

In so far as North America is concerned it is a remarkable fact that all of the explorations and investigations into the antiquity and origin of the primitive races of this continent show that the greatest and highest degree of civilization was attained on the Pacific coast. I will speak more of this later, but in passing it may be fitting to say here that this is an important point in our consideration of the history and ultimate disappearance of the continent of Lemuria and the distribution of its surviving people.

In considering whether the races of man had one common origin or not we must keep in mind the fact that if the races of man originated in one locality and from that point distributed their descendants throughout the world, we must concede that there were ways and means for the journeying of the races of men from one continent to another throughout the world. In this regard we have little difficulty for there is every indication of a reliable nature, that many of the great open spaces now filled with Oceans and bodies of water were at one time occupied by continents and large islands.

We need not resort to the theoretical possibility of man having traveled from Russia and through Asia across the Bering Strait into Alaska, for while there is evidence that men of an Asiatic origin did eventually reach Alaska and leave monuments there proving the fact, nevertheless, there is other evidence to indicate that men reached the shores of America by devious routes in various ages.

On the other hand, in considering the question as to whether man may have originated in various parts of the world simultaneously and without contact or knowledge of the existence of other races in other parts of the world, we have this one very important fact to keep in mind, namely, that investigations and researches including the most carefully made study of the relies found in excavations in all parts of the world show that the primitive or original races existing in each locality started with some culture or development of civilized ideas, and gradually created an original or independent civilization of its own. If all the races of man had one common origin and gradually spread throughout the world we must concede that the migrations would not have begun until man had attained a very high State of civilization and had developed many methods of caring for himself and promoting his best interests. In such a case those who reached foreign lands and established communities of their race on new and virgin soil where no other human beings had ever lived, would naturally have begun their new lives in a new land with a certain degree of advanced culture and advanced forms of civilization.

The rapidly accumulating evidence from all parts of the world proves that this is so. In nearly every case, the earliest relies, the earliest evidences of human occupation indicate some form of civilization and for this reason we have a right to assume that in these localities the races of men did not have their beginnings independent of any other races in any other parts of the world. Consideration must be given, of course, to the results of retrogression in culture in countries widely separated from easy contact with others.

There is a very large amount of evidence that proves conclusively that there was a considerable amount of migration in the early history of this earth. This is especially true of the Pacific coast, of South America, and is an important factor in the study of the mystery of the disappearance of the continent of Lemuria.

Before entering upon a discussion of the existence of the continent of Lemuria and a description of its people and their habits and customs it may be well to State in this first chapter the nature of some of the evidence that has been carefully compiled after being gathered by many men and in many expeditions, all of which I have followed with keen interest. In the first place, it is more than likely that we shall eventually find that the North American Indians are descendants of the "lost tribes of Israel." This belief has gradually developed in the minds of those who have made a careful study of the origin of the American Indians and of their languages, customs, habits, and early products. It may be interesting to my readers to know that one of the outstanding discoveries in this regard was the finding that in all of the various tribes of Indians in America there are certain words that are common to all, although slightly different in sound or symbol. A list of these words common to all of the tribes has shown that they were words which were identical with words used by the tribes known as the Israelites.

When one considers the unusual and enormous diversity of the languages and the tribes of North American Indians and the fact that tribes that lived very near each other were unable to understand each other or to communicate with each other in any form, then the existence of certain common words of an identical nature and meaning become highly significant. In the second place, it has been found that nearly all of these identical words had a religious or mystical meaning and had nothing to do with objects or conditions of a purely local nature, and very often related to principles and laws of a Cosmic nature and pertaining to nothing else in their language or in their customs and habits. In the third place, it was found that there were certain holidays or holy days or ceremonial days that were quite common to all of the tribes despite the great variance in their manner of living, their beliefs, and their tribal philosophy.

Again it was found that most of these ceremonial days had a Cosmic, mystical and religious significance and were coincident with similar holy days prevalent among the "Israelites." Again, considering the fact that many of these Indian tribes were so widely separated that an entire continent lay between them so that they were so unknown to each other that when they were eventually brought into contact with each other they were astounded to know of the existence of the other, we can well realize that the similarity and coincidence of ceremonial days could not be the result of late intercommunication or the recent exchange of ideas.

How the American Indians came to be the descendants of the "lost tribes of Israel" is a matter that requires further investigation and the presentation of the problem would require another separate book. The subject has no special relationship with our study of the continent of Lemuria except that we must keep in mind the fact that the American Indians may represent a portion of the descendants of Lemuria and Atlantis.

That these American Indians could have descended from the Israelites by way of migration across the Pacific is indicated by the fact that many Asiatic dialects and Asiatic evidences have been found in North America and this subject, too, is complete enough to constitute a volume of its own. But there is this significant point in connection with the study of the distribution of the Asiatic dialects and Asiatic distinctions. AU of the Asiatic dialects and Asiatic relies are found only on the Pacific coast, and almost wholly along the north western shore of the North American continent. This becomes highly significant as we shall see later on.

On the other hand, along the western coast of South America we find striking evidence of the identity of tribal words with oceanic dialects, plainly indicating and definitely proving that there was some easy means of access between the western shore of South America and the various people of Oceania. In fact, many of the tribes living along the western shore of South America are surprisingly like the natives of many of the present Pacific Islands both in features and color and in many minute respects. For instance, the Sirionos of Bolivia, constituting an isolated race of primitive people unlike all of the other races of that country but having slightly wavy hair of a very fine texture with large bushy beards and typical Oceanic features resembling no other race anywhere in the world except those of Oceania, are unlike any of the Indian tribes of either North or South America. Furthermore, in some of the expeditions which I have carefully followed and worked with in analytical study of their researches, there has been unearthed along the California coast certain prehistoric graves in which were found adzes, axe-heads, and other stone articles carefully made, and in a style and manner typical of the work of some of the tribes still existing on islands in the Pacific Ocean, and made of stone that is found no where else except in those islands of the Pacific Ocean.

It must be kept in mind that these islands now existing in the Pacific are unquestionably the remnants of other islands and a large continent which once occupied the space or part of the space of the Pacific Ocean, and unless we concede that ancient men did sail or journey by some means for many months from distant islands in the Pacific to the western shore of South America, we must admit that there must have been other islands or large bodies of land in the Pacific close to South America and which were occupied by tribes like unto those still existing on the Pacific islands and with stone similar to that still found on such islands. In such a case it would have been a simple matter for the pre-historic tribes to have journeyed from the one continent on the Pacific to the other and to have made such migrations at a time when the Pacific continent was slowly submerging.

Another interesting point is the fact that North America affords the greatest study in the investigation of the origin of man because, even excluding the many American Indian tribes with their various dialects, customs, and habits, we still have evidence in North America of other tribes of distinctly different dialects and habits. In fact, the variation of races, of dialects, and customs, was unquestionably greater in this new world than it ever was in the old world, and so far as the Pacific coast is concerned, more than one hundred distinct languages or dialects were spoken by the various tribes within a few square miles, constituting a greater number of distinct tribes for the same amount of country than in any other part of this world. Even at the time that North America was first visited by explorers the condition of variation in tongue and character was highly impressive. Many of the natives were naked and savage; others were nomads. Other tribes were partly civilized. Some were agriculturists; some were hunters. Some dwelt in the open fields and valleys in the shelter of the brush and trees, while others had built their homes of adobe and the skins of animals using methods found in no other parts of the world, or using methods, customs, and habits that were identical with other tribes in other parts of the world. Most of the tribes evidenced a progressiveness in development to the stone age indicating that they had advanced beyond all the primitive states. Some of these tribes had already reached a very high State of culture and had attained real artistic skill, and many of them had accomplished feats which had never been excelled or equaled by any of the other races in the history of the world.

I am referring particularly to the Pacific coast where the early explorers were astonished to find among primitive races and primitive people the evidence of a very high civilization.

It is true that in the Yucatan there was found much evidence of a highly civilized race with a very remarkable development in culture, but this is the story of the Mayans, a race of people who descended from the Atlanteans and Lemurians intermarried, when the continent of Atlantis submerged in the Atlantic Ocean. This, too, is another story in the history of man that has no bearing upon the story of the Lemurians but the fact that the Mayan writing is one of the most marvelous achievements of any race and is known only in its most perfected form, and must have required thousands of years for development, indicates how a cultured and civilized race of people came to this North American continent to live among primitive conditions.

Certainly this gives us a picture of the polyglot of races of man, the mixtures of civilization, the variance of culture, and the wide dissemination of man himself on a continent in the new world, as it is called today, but which we shall see was really an old world before Europe had become even partly civilized.

In the book of Genesis we have a story of the origin of man that is not only symbolical but in some passages quite historical. We must bear in mind, however, that the story given to us in Genesis is the result of age-old traditions passed from person to person by word of mouth for many ages before becoming recorded in the crude writings on stones. Then such stories were later rearranged and re-worded for preservation in manuscripts, and still later re-arranged, edited, and prepared for translation into other languages and for wider dissemination. The stories, therefore, of the origin of man and especially of the great flood, are not mythical stories but historical facts known to all ages of man as part of the traditions of man's history. Geology and the study of the earth's surface and a study of all of the things within the earth give us mute but indisputable evidence of the fact that at one time great floods did destroy most if not all of the living things on the face of the earth, and that as the flood came to various parts of the world there were migrations and the movement of hordes of people from one country to another. The flood was not simultaneous everywhere but gradual throughout a long period of time with one continent or another gradually disappearing here and there. There is scarcely a tribe of people in any part of the world that has not a story of a great flood among its traditions. The early visitors and explorers who came to the shores of America were astonished to find that the tribes living here in such great isolation and separated from all other parts of the world with no means of communication or contact with the traditions of the Orientals, had their own stories of a great flood that were identical with the stories told in Genesis and held by the people of Asia and other parts of the Orient. How this story of the world flood came to the American Indians and the hundreds of other tribes here was a puzzle, indeed, to the early explorers, but today there is no more mystery about it and the explanation of the possible means of such knowledge constitutes a part of our study.

We have been accustomed to think that man's first appearance in America was not many years before the coming of Columbus or the early explorers. I am speaking now of years in a relative manner, for a few hundred years, or a few thousand years, constitute a short time compared With the existence of the races of man. But the researches within recent years, by every department of geology and the study of man, have set back man's presence in America many thousands of years. Some years ago no one would have believed that human beings dwelt in America more than twenty thousand years ago. Today we have proof that is indisputable that man not only inhabited North America thousands of years ago, but that the races of man existing in this country at that time were the equal if not actually the superior of the races of man in the old world at the same time. I have in mind the exhibits from the gravel deposits in Frederick, Oklahoma, and in Raton, New Mexico, where we have seen articles that were buried and associated with animals known to have lived only in very ancient times. Such animals were mastodons, camels, horses, elephants, ground sloths and others. Underneath the fossils were found flint arrow-heads and spear heads and other human-made articles, and some of these were buried in the bodies of the animals and were still attached to the bones of these animals who had been killed with them, and these animals are indisputably and scientifically recognized as belonging to very ancient periods. In at least fifty localities in North America such exhibits have been found. The most definite proof was found at Colorado, Texas, where flint weapons which had undoubtedly killed the animals were within the skeletons or embedded in the bones. Every scientist and profound student of the subject of the origin of man in America will tell you that the evidence is rapidly piling up and while some of these may not admit with me the existence of Lemuria as a separate continent with its own race of people, they will admit that people came to America many, many thousands of years ago from some unknown country in the west.

FASCINATING INCIDENTS OF THE PAST

The idea that there have been a number of continents which disappeared in ages gone by is very old and is found expressed in various ways in the oldest legends of many lands. There are references in many ancient writings to tribes of people living toward the east or toward the west in localities that are now occupied with seas and Oceans.

I must avoid the subject of the continent of Atlantis as much as possible because that lost continent has been well dealt with in the book by Ignatius Donnelly and by others and because as a story, not as fascinating as that of Lemuria, would occupy a complete volume in itself. But, for many centuries the idea of a lost continent having once existed in the space now occupied by the Atlantic Ocean was expressed in hundreds of manuscripts and books, though considered often as merely a legend without scientific foundation. Even when Sir Francis Bacon wrote his famous book called "The New Atlantis" and thereby gave some weight to the old stories of a lost Atlantis, many still believed that the ancient continent was as mythical as the New World he described. Along with the coming of the realization that the new Atlantis described by Bacon was a prophetic picture of the

United States and Canada, also came a realization, through scientific discoveries, that the lost Atlantis might be more fact than fable.

In recent years, however, all doubt about a submerged continent at the bottom of the Atlantic Ocean has been cast aside, for the great scientific explorations and tests have revealed that there is such a continent, and that at one time it undoubtedly filled most of the space between the shores of the New World and the Old World in the temperate zone. The Azores Islands and the Madeira Islands are now generally accepted to be mountain peaks of the ancient Atlantis continent still lifting their heads above the Oceans surface. That there were other such islands in the Atlantic in centuries gone by is now generally believed because of the many references to them in ancient writings.

The disappearance of the continent of Atlantis, however, is only one incident in the history of the changes that have taken place on the surface of this earth. It is more than likely that at one time there was far more land than water, and because of the picturesqueness of the subject I wish to deal lightly and briefly with some of the great changes that unquestionably took place. It is impossible in a book of this kind and in a limited chapter of this nature to speak of all of these changes in detail.

First of all, we cannot exactly determine how large the continent of Atlantis really was, but, of course, we can be sure it came in contact with North America and Africa. It may appear as though this would indicate that the continent of Atlantis must have been very large, but we will anticipate that argument by stating that there are other good scientific reasons for believing that the continental shores of North America as we know them today and the shores of the European coast were not as widely separated as at the present time. First of all we have evidence to show that the coast lines of both continents have been gradually changing, just as they are changing today. Despite the many places in which man has filled in, with earth and other material, various points and places along each coast and especially along the North American shore, the washing away of the earth and the disappearance of part of the land along the Ocean has been more rapid and more exhaustive than we realize at first consideration. Many of the very ancient maps that show discrepancies between the present coast lines of North America and Europe are not the result of error, but fairly accurate pictures of what the coast line was at one time.

We have no reason to assume that a continent is something that is anchored and fastened to the center of a great sphere and is immovable. Small islands have shifted as well as disappeared and reappeared in times past and it is possible for an entire continent to move either eastward or westward or even toward the north or south or twist itself slightly diagonally. Scientists now believe that because a continent can float and move on the surface of the earth that very likely the North American continent was a part of the European continent and that the two present shore lines of the North American and European side were once the shore lines of a river that merely divided certain parts of a great continent, and that gradually the river widened because of the movement of the continents and continued to do so until the river became an Ocean.

One of the points held forth to justify this idea was the fact that not only did the continents move but that the rugged and peculiar Eastern shore line of the North American continent seemed to have a similar contour to the western shore line of the European continent, and in fact there is such a similarity despite some discrepancies. It is scientifically possible that during the many and marvelous changes that have taken place on the surface of this earth and while an entire continent of ice changed into a continent of grass and trees, changing even the very surface of the earthly substances themselves, there may have arisen a great mass of land in the Atlantic Ocean after the two continents, or the two half's of one continent, had separated and formed two independent continental bodies.

Among the other picturesque changes is that of the creation of the present Gulf of Mexico. Undoubtedly at one time the present Gulf of Mexico did not exist as a body of water but as a deep and beautiful valley lying between, or nearly completely surrounded by, high mountain regions. The present peninsula of Florida is not a part of such mountain regions rising above water but an accumulation of sand, coral, and shells which have been deposited on the upper peaks and surface of a sunken mountain chain. In other words, at one time the chain of mountains known as the Appalachians was continued on southward in a line to meet what is now the West Indian Islands and on to South America, or another mountain chain began just north of Florida and continued downward to the West Indian Islands and South America. Such a mountain chain would have enclosed a large valley lying between it and the present eastern shore of Mexico with its mountainous regions, for we find that it is a mountain chain that constitutes the only present connection between North and South America through which the Panama Canal has been cut. The present Caribbean Sea, as well as the Gulf of Mexico, would have been within this valley. While the Islands of the West Indies are really composed of parts of the ancient mountain chain, still above the surface of the water, the land of Florida is a newly composed material accumulated in time, as things from the sea are accustomed to accumulate around anything to which they can anchor themselves.

Undoubtedly the present Mississippi River flowed through the center of this ancient valley and had an outlet somewhere near the Islands of Martinique and Barbados. Into this valley spread the survivors of the lost continent of Atlantis, for there are some islands of the West Indies group, such as those just mentioned, which indicate that they were once in close contact with the people of the lost continent of Atlantis. As time made its changes in this valley and it began to sink lower than the sea level, and no longer carried the water of the Mississippi off into the Atlantic Ocean, it gradually became filled with an inland sea and this in turn became the great gulf with the continuous sinking of the eastern mountain range which separated it from the Atlantic Ocean.

The descendants of Atlantis and Lemuria living in this peaceful valley gradually migrated to the sides and top of the mountain ranges both east and west. Eventually those who had migrated to the mountains on the eastern side now lying beneath the peninsula of Florida had to migrate again, and some went south to the mountain peaks now constituting the West Indian Islands, while the others went westward and upon the highest land accessible to them they once again built their temples and their homes, this time more permanently than ever because of belief in the permanency of the new site. Thus we find in the Yucatan and the countries of Guatemala, Honduras, Salvador, Nicaragua and parts of Mexico, the very wonderful temples attributed to the race known as the Mayans, whose structures are scientifically admitted to be older than those in Egypt.

This story of the Mayans is also one that is too great and too interesting to condense into a brief chapter of this book and perhaps some day the marvelous truths and knowledge of the Mayan people will be presented in a separate volume.

Another remarkable change in North America is that of the gradual disappearance and evaporation of the great inland sea that one time occupied the en tire central area of the United States. The Great Lakes, the Mississippi Valley, and the great desert region lying between the Mississippi and the Rocky Mountains were due to terrific though gradual changes in the rising of the land. But even these changes are not as remarkable as another change in the North American continent to which I will refer in a moment.

Going further north we find evidences to indicate that Alaska and Siberia were at one time united and probably the land was broken through and the continents separated by the onrush of ice in the time of the change from the glacial period to the next period, and even north of this there is definite evidence that the country of Canada was once a high plateau continuing far beyond the 70th degree of latitude. Greenland and Canada were originally united and the many islands now composing the Arctic archipelago composed one united land reaching far into the north.

Going into the old world we find many similar examples of changes, as for instance the separation between Africa and Arabia and the separation that is still taking place between Arabia and Persia. The present China Sea and the Gulf of Siam now occupy a place that once constituted a very beautiful valley closed in by a mountain region on the east which now constitutes the Island of Formosa, the Philippine Islands, and the Islands of Borneo, Sumatra and the Malay Peninsula.

We are not concerned at the present time with the Old World and its changes which are far more recent than those of the so called New World, and which are continuing more rapidly in their present day changes than are the changes of North and South America. The

Pacific Ocean is today a great area of continuous changes. The changes in the earth's surface seem to be periodically in zones. From observations I have made over a number of years I firmly believe that the zones of changes are in parallels running westward and eastward; that is to say, like the degrees of longitude. In other words, these parallel zones are at right angles to the equator. In each zone certain changes take place and then the changes move westward to the next zone and complete their work and then move on again westwardly to the next zone. The period of time occupied by each set of changes in each zone is now being studied from a theoretical point of view in order to check up with the periodical changes discovered in the earth's surface by geologists and scientists of various schools of investigation. If this theory is proved to be true and more evidence as convincing as that already found is discovered in the next few years, we will undoubtedly find that part of the Pacific Ocean is at the present time being affected by some of these changes and that these changes will gradually move westward across the continents of Asia and Australia and eventually reach Europe and Africa. The many recent earthquakes off the coast of Asia and Australia indicate that the zone of changes is gradually approaching these continents, and looking back over the history of the changes that have occurred in the Pacific Ocean we find that within the last few hundred years many changes have taken place in a zone that included the Philippine Islands and the thousands of islands north and south of them. This is probably the 20th or 30th time that such changes have taken place in the Pacific Ocean. In other words, the 20th or 30th time that the zones of changes have moved from the east to the west across the entire surface of the earth. The changes that take place are accompanied by earthquakes, terrific storms and cyclones, tidal waves and fires and extreme changes of temperature. There would seem to be also a movement of land along with the movement of the zones of change, and this would account for the continents of North and South America moving away from the continents of Europe and Africa after they had once been divided by water. It would account, also, for the continuous movement of these continents and for the rising of a new continent and its eventual submersion. Keeping in mind that more than half of North America was at one time beneath the water, as well as other parts of it far above the water, and that which was above is below and that which was below is now above, we can see how wonderfully the surface of the earth is being remade and modified. The gradual changes in climate, often blamed upon tidal waves, earthquakes, and Ocean currents, is simply another manifestation of the zone changes referred to above. The changes in climate seem to follow in separate zones after the other changes have taken place or sometimes precede the other changes. There are those who remember many such changes in climate as, for instance, those who recall that in our own lifetime the climate along the north eastern States of the United States was entirely different than what it is today, with winters that began very early in the fall and were extremely cold and white with snow before Christmas, whereas today New York, for example, seldom experiences heavy snow storms until almost the beginning of spring or certainly not before February or March. If such a great change could take place in the lifetime of one generation we may well understand how such a change could have taken place as would have altered the eastern states from being completely covered with snow and ice throughout the entire year to moderate temperature and warm weather most of the year. Similar changes in climate are taking place along the Pacific coast at the present time, definitely modifying the temperature and improving the climate of northern and central California especially.

Many interesting geographical changes have been made through these zone effects and, of course, it is reasonable to say that the results of these changes are responsible for some of our national and international boundaries. The British Isles for instance are powerful in their present position solely as a result of the changes that have taken place in centuries gone by. Very often picturesque effects have resulted from such changes, such as the magnificent Niagara Falls and some of the wonderful falls in Southern Africa. Then, again, Manhattan Island in New York is an example of how nature can contribute to the fortune of man. Manhattan Island was at one time a part of the mainland and was suddenly cut off as though a huge knife had sliced off an edge of the mainland and pushed the slice away leaving a river in the space between. A study of the Palisades along the Hudson River would convince anyone that some terrific earthquake or volcano has split the solid rock of the mainland in almost a straight line, and the slice that was thus separated from the larger body dropped several hundred feet into the Ocean to form a peninsula floating in the Ocean at a lower level than the mainland. This peninsula finally broke loose from its upper connection and became an island, and is the most valuable island in the world.

The Great Salt Lake of Utah is a remnant of an enormous inland sea that covered hundreds of miles in each direction filling the valley that lies between the Rocky Mountains and the foot-hills of the Sierra Nevada range. The gradual evaporation and condensation of the water for many centuries is responsible for the saltiness of the present remaining water. Marks on the side of the rocks surrounding the present lake plainly show the original height of the surface of this sea and also show the gradual lowering of that level throughout many centuries.

All of the foregoing changes, representing only a fraction of those that might be pointed out, are far less surprising than one great change that has taken place on the Pacific coast of North America and which enables us to understand much about the disappearance of the continent of Lemuria and the migration of its race of people.

In order that this important change may be thoroughly understood the reader is urged to study the maps and illustrations presented in this book so that a proper registration of the pictorial effect may be made in the consciousness.

First of all we must take into consideration that the Pacific coast of the United States, as it now exists, represents the unity of two continents. Every student of geology and every expert in the study of the soil, the flora, the minerals and the relies of the races of man has come face to face with the many mysteries of the Pacific coast. The whole region of that coast from Vancouver to Lower California presents distinctive and unvarying differences of soil, flora, minerals and relies of nature and the races of man unlike anything found in the mid-west of the continent. In other words, the land lying between the eastern foothills of the Sierra Nevada mountains to the shore line along the

Pacific Ocean, is distinctly different in all of its exhibits from the land that lies east of the Sierra Nevada foothills or the foothills of the Cascade range. Here, in this narrow strip of land, averaging about three hundred to five hundred miles in width and several thousand miles in length we have soil, products of the soil, along with relies of man, representing the oldest surface of the earth ever discovered by scientific investigation. Here the oldest living things known to man still remain, such as giant redwood trees that are at least three thousand years old, with relies of other trees that lived and grew to great age many, many, thousands of years previously. In fact, the flora of this land was so abundant for so many thousands of years that the soil today is filled with and partly composed of the decayed flora that has accumulated for so many centuries that it constitutes the most fertile and the most productive soil in the world, and everything that will grow in soil anywhere in the world will grow in this soil prolifically and to unusual development. Immediately east of the Sierra Nevada Mountains and the Cascade Range the soil is entirely different and all of its products are different.

A close study covering a very long period, resulting in the finding of many exhibits of nature and the handicraft of man along with the remains of many species of animal life, proves conclusively that between the Sierra Nevada Mountains and the Cascade Range and the Rocky Mountains, or in other words in that great valley that lies between these two great ranges there was a body of water covering the soil and separating the mountain ranges for many centuries. In other words, if we imagine that the Gulf of California, which now separates Baja California from Mexico, was continued on northward through the valley of the Colorado River and up into the district of the Great Salt Lake and then on through Idaho, parts of Washington, and Montana into Canada, we would have a complete separation of the Pacific part of the continent from the mid-west as shown on a map herewith. There probably were many islands rising in this body of water at some period of the past, but ages ago this great Ocean separated the Rocky Mountains from the present coast range of the North American continent.

The coast range, the Sierras, the Cascades, and the present valleys of California, Oregon, and Washington, were part of another continent that rose in the Pacific Ocean west of the original continent of North America. This other continent of which we now have only a relic was the continent of Lemuria.

To understand what occurred we must realize that continents and islands have not only completely submerged in the centuries that have passed but in some instances have only partially submerged, and large islands have dipped or tipped to one side or one end, while the other end has risen higher into the space above the water, just like a large piece of wood floating upon the surface of the water and being pushed downward on one end; there would be a tendency to have the opposite end rise slightly and especially so if at the time of the change that caused the dipping or tipping of the land there were such eruptions and earthquakes and other natural changes in the surface of the earth as would have pushed up one end while causing another end to dip into the water. From a study of many ancient maps and a study of deep sea explorations we find many parts of islands that are under water having every indication of one time being far above water, and we have the reverse condition in many places where study of the flora and soil and the remaining rocks show that in ages gone by they were covered with water for a long time and have only recently, comparatively speaking, risen from their watery cradle.

From every investigation that has been made and the closest study of the nature of the Pacific Ocean and its islands, and from the deep sea soundings and study of the flora of the Pacific Ocean, it is very evident that the continent of Lemuria occupied a great area and was probably a continent as large as the North American continent if not considerably larger. It unquestionably reached from 0 degrees Southern latitude to 40 or 50 northern latitude, and fro. A close proximity to North America to a close proximity to the continent of Africa. The New Zealand group of islands and all of the other thousands of large and small islands in the Pacific Ocean are mountain peak remnants of the submerged continent.

There are indications that the eastern shore of this ancient continent was close enough to the North American continent to permit of migration and some form of transportation long before Lemuria submerged. When the continent submerged, however, the extreme eastern edge of it which was very mountainous and very high above the sea level remained partly above water and the changes that took place during that cataclysm caused the continent of North America to move westwards until the mountain ranges which remained above water united with the rising land of the western part of the North American continent. This brought the great valley lying between the Rocky Mountain range and the Cascade and Sierra Ranges above sea level and made one continuous piece of dry land except for the inland sea in the Salt Lake region.

We must bear in mind that most of the separated continents, as we look upon them in present day maps, are united beneath the water of the Ocean. A study of the flora of the Ocean would show, for instance, that the present Gulf of Mexico is merely a deep valley into which the waters of the Atlantic have rushed and that the continent of South America is connected with the continent of North America by much more land than the mere peninsula through which the Panama Canal has been cut. Undoubtedly the submerged continent of Lemuria is connected with part of the continent of North America beneath the Ocean.

We are inclined to think of rivers being formed by the flow of water down the mountain sides and eating away the soil in the mad rush to find an outlet to the Ocean or to a lake or some other form of dispersion, but until nature forms a valley or a continuously declining surface into which the draining water of the mountains can naturally flow a river cannot form itself. In some cases earthquakes and surface changes in mountainous regions have caused a spreading of the rocks creating a canyon in the midst of mountains into which the waters of the mountains will pour and form a river. The Grand Canyons of Colorado are unquestionably a living testimony to the cataclysmic changes that took place at the time the continent of Lemuria was submerged and the waters lying between the Rocky mountains and the Sierras and Cascade mountains were emptied into the Pacific to make room for the rising land of the present valleys and desert places.

By studying the maps in this book, therefore, one will see that the western portion of the United States is a remnant of the submerged continent of Lemuria and that here we have the oldest of living things, the oldest of cultivated soil, and the most numerous relies of the human race which had reached a higher state of cultural development and civilization than any other races of man. It will be interesting, therefore, to examine some of these wonderful exhibits of antiquity as discovered in California and other parts of western America and see the real proofs that Nature has preserved for us.

MYSTERIOUS FORCES OF THE UNIVERSE

*I*n Order to understand some of the mighty changes that took place in the surface of the earth in ages gone by, I believe it well to present here, in very brief form, a panoramic picture or description of what occurred in the past two hundred thousand years.

I will not take the time nor space to quote authors or records for the statements made in this chapter, but will refer to these in a separate part of the book. Suffice it to say that where archaeological and geological records do not give some of these facts, ancient writings, carvings, and engravings on stone supply the deficiencies in an indisputable manner.

Beginning, then, at the earliest period of which we have any definite knowledge, we find that two hundred thousand years ago the surface of the earth was very much like that pictured in map No. 1. The large dark portions shown on this map constitute one unbroken continent reaching from the 20th degree of eastern longitude to the 80th degree of western longitude, and occupying a large population of the present Pacific Ocean and lapping over into Asia and Africa. This continent was the only habitable land sufficiently above water to have any considerable degree of vegetation. The shaded portion shown on the map, which represents the ancient continent of North and South America and the present continents of Asia and Africa, was either wholly submerged beneath the water or it was a form of swamp land known to the inhabitants of the continent of Lemuria but not available for habitations of any kind.

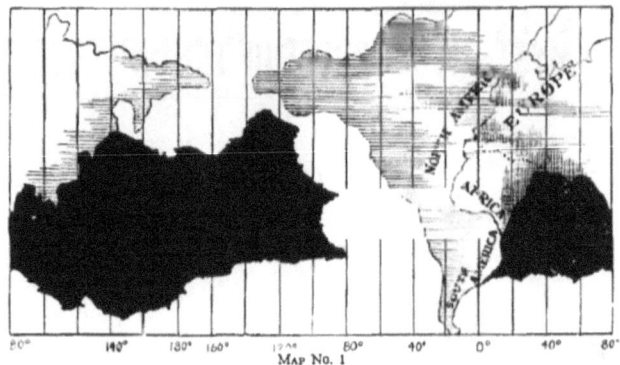

Map No. 1

At least one hundred and fifty thousand years ago these partially submerged lands were known and described and sometimes pictured in maps, from which the map shown herewith has been taken. But, for many thousands of years, these swampy lands were unpopulated and considered as barren and useless. There must have been parts of this swampy land that were higher than others and, from some indications, we find that those portions, shaded a little darker than the others on the map, were known as *highlands*, but still of little value.

On the one continent shown in black on the map, all human civilization began, and, probably, here too, was the beginning of all creatures that lived out of or above the waters of the earth. This ancient continent, which is now called Lemuria, but which had other names in times that are past, was truly the *cradle of the human race* and the original Garden of Eden, if we look upon the ancient traditional story of the creation of man as symbolical of the actual facts. In all ancient records and among all tribes of people there is a trace of this same old story of the creation of man in a Garden of Eden, and like many others in the Old Testament of the present day Bible, these symbolical, traditional stories are evidences of great truths passed down from generation to generation of the human race.

For one hundred thousand years or more the cradle of civilization on the ancient continent of Lemuria rocked the newly born of many tribes which descended from the earliest created beings, and it may be said, in passing, that the earliest records indicate that man was created coincident with the creation of other living creatures, and that he was not a descendant from any lower specie of the animal kingdom, but always of human form and expression and with dominant control over the other creatures around him. Thus, the old Biblical story, representing the ancient traditions of the history of man, appear to be correct and indicate that God created man immediately after having created the other creatures over whom he was to have dominion.

Just about a hundred thousand years ago great changes began to take place on the surface, and below the surface, of the lands and waters of this earth. I shall not take time to speak of the facts about gas belts, volcanoes, and other causes of earthquakes, temblors and shocks, which periodically affected the surface of the earth in such a definite manner as to make it evident that the earth was passing through a regular and continuous program of evolutionary changes, for the science of archaeology and geology are replete with traditions and interesting descriptions of the causes and nature of such periodic changes. Suffice it to say, in this regard, that these changes appear to have been cyclic* (see appendix 1) and to have moved in waves like magnetic waves from the east toward the west, and each wave covered a narrow band of the earth's surface much like the bands of longitude shown on the maps herewith. These bands were evidently about forty to eighty degrees of longitude in width and extended from the north to the south poles. They were truly magnetic in effect for their results are indelibly recorded in the matter and elements that compose the hard and dry substances of the earth's surface and show that great heat of an electric and magnetic nature often instantaneously reduced the hardest materials to molten. Sometimes such changes occurred in two opposite parts of the earth's surface at the same time, but the changes were in progressive steps across the surface of the earth from east to west.

Our continents, as we know them today, therefore, have grown to what they are through the many changes that have taken place and they are continuing to grow and to change. Coast lines of all continents are varying from century to century and new islands rise and disappear in various parts of the world. Mountains have changed their height; valleys have been raised or lowered; seas have come and disappeared and even climatic conditions have changed in the western world, as well as in the eastern world.

It is interesting to note that in the processes of the development and growth of continents on the surface of this earth that all lands began as swampy marshes and either raised slowly in parts or were left higher through the waters receding in a gradual manner, or were pushed upwards in places by sudden submarine or other explosions; but, practically all of the continents in their early stages were more or less level, and high mountains were entirely unknown, for mountains are a very recent addition to all continents.

A hundred thousand years ago, when the present European and adjoining continental lands were beginning to be higher and dryer, there were very few high places that might be called hills and absolutely no mountains at all. Even Lemuria, the oldest of the continents and the one which was at this time well populated and thickly covered with vegetation, had little or no hills and absolutely no mountains.

About eighty-two thousand years ago the first of the definitely recorded series of magnetic waves began to move once more around the earth's circuit from east to west. The ones which had preceded these by several hundred thousand years, are not definitely recorded, but those which began about eighty-two thousand years ago affected civilization to such an extent and made such important changes in the lands that were highly civilized, that records regarding the changes were made. We find that the first and most important change that took place is that shown on map No. 2. First, beginning at about 140 degrees eastern longitude, the part of the continent of Lemuria that was connected with Asia and Africa began to sink slightly enough to be broken up into swampy islands, and other parts of it submerged leaving the continent of Lemuria a much smaller continent, located entirely in the Pacific Ocean and contacting some of the present day islands near the shore of Asia. As the magnetic waves and degree of changes passed eastward, the continent of Europe rose higher and ceased to be a swamp-land and became high and dry desert wastes with a few inland seas, as shown on the map. Rivers were formed in the lowest of the sections of the lands and as the magnetic waves continued further eastward large rivers were formed which separated or divided parts of Europe into several continents. Map No. 2 shows the European continents shaded in a manner to separate them. The large black portion forming one entire continent from the north to the south, and reaching from about 20 degrees eastern longitude to 130 western longitude, is the land that was destined to become North and South America. This great continent, shown in black, rose very high, and rapidly became covered with heavy vegetation, while the rest of Europe, shown in shaded lines, and all of Africa, remained desert land, with most of Asia still swampy land.

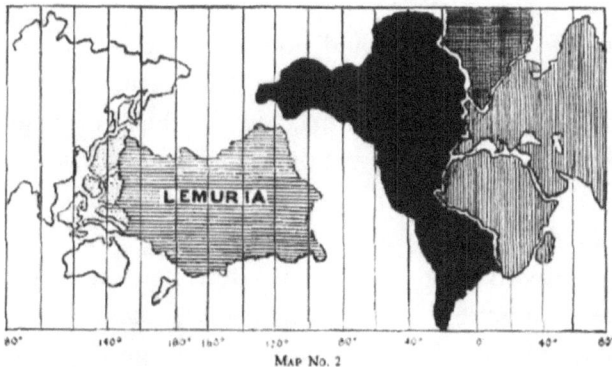
Map No. 2

The people of Lemuria now began to colonize, and the records indicate that about eighty thousand years ago they began to make pilgrimages to other lands, sending sufficient numbers in each pilgrimage to constitute a colony or community. The first experiments of this kind were directed toward Asia, but many pilgrimages were made both easterly and westerly.

About seventy-five thousand years ago the continent in black, shown on Map No. 2, began to drift and to separate itself from the rest of Europe and Africa. To those who may wonder whether it is possible for a continent to drift or not, let me say that there are many and sufficient proofs in the sciences of archaeology and geology to show that this is possible; not all land on the surface of the earth is a part of the submarine floor or body of the earth. Even when continents are attached to the body of the earth these continents can be moved and have moved through the changes in the surface of the earth, caused by earthquakes and cataclysms of various kinds. It appears from a careful study of the nature of the earth, as a sphere, that there must be internal regions of great space filled with great heat and gases. It is apparent that in some of the cataclysms that have taken place, land has been swallowed up by the vast internal spaces of the earth, as well as having submerged just beneath the surface of the water, for all of the continents that have disappeared, and all of the islands that have lowered beneath the surface of the water are not discoverable through deep sea exploration. As I shall point out later, the sinking of some of these continents has caused a lowering of the level of the ocean's surface. The sinking of a continent just beneath the surface of the Ocean would not cause the waters to materially drop in their height, inasmuch as the displacement of water by the sinking of the continent would make up for the absence of the continent in the surface of the water. Some continents, however, and many islands, have been drawn completely into the very bowels of the earth and have not displaced any of the water at all.

In keeping with the magnetic pulsations and earthquakes moving in an easterly direction around the earth, the continent that became North and South America moved westerly in a gradual manner, separating itself entirely from Europe, Africa, and Greenland, and at the same time leaving a unique coast-line for Europe and Africa. Students of geography have noticed for many years that the eastern shore line of North and South America was very similar to the western shore line of Greenland, Europe, and Africa, and that the pieces of continent could be fitted together much like the pieces of a cut-out puzzle, making due allowances for the ever continuing changes of shore lines. At the same time that these changes were taking place mountains were beginning to grow in the form of small hills, and the people of Lemuria were continuing their colonizations in other lands.

About fifty thousand years ago other very important changes were noted by those who made any official records or permanent writings of any kind. We find the surface of the earth much like that shown in Map No. 3. The continents of North and South America had moved westerly and had gone as far as they could go, inasmuch as the western shore of North America had reached and contacted the easterly shore of Lemuria, and that part now known as Alaska had reached and was contacting the easterly limits of Asia. At the same time we find that a new continent was beginning to rise in the Atlantic, and swamp lands appeared there, contacting and uniting North America with the shore of Europe and Africa.

The reader should keep in mind that it does not take a very great cataclysm to make many important changes in regard to continents and islands. Only recently it was determined by deep sea soundings and under sea explorations that if the entire land surface of the earth should be caused to raise above four thousand feet, or a little less than a mile, every continent on the face of the earth would be connected by land above water. In other words, when another great cataclysm occurs, and it should be in the nature of explosions that would raise the land only four thousand feet, all of the continents of the world would be in touch with each other above the surface of the water and thereby afford dry land communication and transportation. Think what a mighty change in the world would result from this! And, it may be said in passing, a cataclysm that would raise or lower the surface of continents or lands only four or five thousand feet would be a small cataclysm, indeed, compared to those that have taken place in the past. Therefore, we should not be surprised to learn that about fifty thousand years ago this new continent suddenly appeared above the surface of the water. Whether it had been in submarine existence at the time the North and South American continent rode over it in its westerly journey, or whether it was pushed entirely from the bowels of the earth upward for many miles cannot be determined, since little of it remains to this day.

Along with the rising of this continent of Atlantis the continent of South and North America also rose to a considerable height and mountains rose higher. Where marshy lands were thus enclosed by highlands deep seas were formed, and lakes and rivers. By studying map No. 3 the reader will note that the bay of Hudson was at one time a great sea connected with the St. Lawrence River and the Lakes, and that the Mississippi Valley had a very wide river connecting with an inland sea or lake in the Colorado Valley, and that between the Sierra Nevada Mountains and the Rocky Mountains there was another great inland sea covering what is now known as the State of Utah. Another sea was formed in South America in the valley of the Amazon. In fact, records show that boats from Lemuria and from the west were able to sail into this sea and out again into the Atlantic Ocean, and that international communication and pilgrimages from east to west were made by this route. This would have made the lower part of South America a separate continent, as shown on the map.

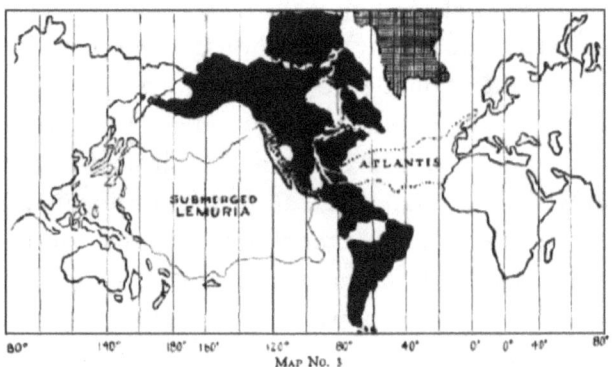

Map No. 3

Greenland was caught midway in its westerly movement and remained fixed where it is today, although the northern part of North America was not broken up into islands but formed several large continents.

The most important consideration, however, is to be given to the western coast of North America. As the continent of North America moved westward it joined with the eastern high coast of Lemuria, which was the first part of Lemuria to have its hills rise to great heights and become real mountains. Later on when the continent of Lemuria was submerged this high portion of Lemuria, joining the western part of North America, remained above the water and constitutes the Pacific coast of North America, including the States of Washington, Oregon, all of California, a small part of Nevada, Lower California, and parts of Arizona and Mexico. The western end of Lemuria, near the coast of Asia, was beginning to sink and form islands, and here was the beginning of the formation of the new or separate continent of Australia and the islands east and north of it. In Europe mountains were beginning to rise and in Lemuria itself civilization was reaching a great height of development and the people were attaining mastership in a sense not even comprehended by us today; for their civilization was now fully a hundred and fifty thousand years old, whereas our present civilization is still a child in comparison.

Approximately twenty-five thousand years ago, further important changes took place on the surface of the earth. The continent of Atlantis rose higher and mountains began to form on it, especially in the eastern section, and mountains were forming rapidly in Europe in and around the Mediterranean Sea or north of it, and across the French and Spanish peninsula. The shore line of Europe and Africa was gradually changing through the disappearance of islands and the washing away of swamp-lands along its edges, leaving the continent of Atlantis separated from both Europe and Africa.

North and South America were also passing through changes, for the land was rising in South America to form mountains, and new mountains forming the Rocky Mountain range were rising, narrowing some of the seas to a smaller area, closing the rivers to a narrow stream, and closing the Amazon sea in South America to a river in a dry valley. As the western coast of Atlantis began to change and separate itself from North America, islands were formed and parts of the continent at Bering Strait were seriously affected, as well as the small continents north of Canada, now composed of islands.

Lemuria itself was continuing to sink in the western portion, forcing all of the people to move to parts of Asia, Australia, and the islands of the Pacific, or to the eastern part of the continent bordering upon the shores of North and South America. The continent of Atlantis had become peopled with pilgrims and colonists from Lemuria, who had crossed North and South America. Many parts of

South America and many parts of North America were also peopled by tribes descended from the early pilgrims from Lemuria.

Approximately eighteen thousand years ago Atlantis was at its height in civilization. The eastern part of its continent now had enormous mountains and toward the west there were civilized areas covered with mountains rising to great heights. The people from Lemuria had reached Africa in their westerly journeys and had settled along the shores of the Red Sea and the Nile River, which was a very wide river feeding a number of lakes and inland seas and thereby affording excellent vegetation and the conveniences and necessities for civilization. This was the beginning of Egyptian civilization.

Three thousand years later, or approximately fifteen thousand years ago, another great cataclysm occurred which greatly changed the Southern part of North America. The people from Lemuria had settled in and around the rivers and great seas in what is now known as Texas and parts of Mexico and Yucatan. It was natural for these colonists to establish communities where water and vegetation were most abundant and where there would naturally be highlands or mountains acting as watersheds and affording the new product called stone and marble, from which homes could be constructed or into which caves or protected places could be carved or cut. But the great cataclysm of fifteen thousand years ago suddenly came upon the continent of Atlantis and caused the western part of it to sink and at the same time the great valley just north of Mexico and through which the great river known as the Mississippi flowed submerged, destroying almost all of the civilization centered in that part of North America. These people were known under the general name of Mayas, which was a general term given to all of the Lemurians and some of the Atlanteans who had entered that valley and built temples and large cities. The result of this submerging of land formed the present Gulf of Mexico. The peninsula of Florida did not exist at this time, but a few mountain peaks rose where the peninsula of Florida now is and the islands of

Cuba, Porto Rico, and the other islands of the West Indies group were left as remnants of the sinking land. The newly formed mountains of North America that reached down to South America prevented North and South America from becoming separated and formed the present Isthmus, while that part of the old valley that was the highest, because of its great mountains, became the present land of Yucatan, while the rising land that forced the inland sea to disappear became part of the states of Texas, Arizona, and surrounding territory.

The civilization in Atlantis was at its height at this time and the records show that Queen Moo was ruling over the people that had survived and had joined those who lived in the mountains of the Yucatan.

Three thousand years later, or approximately twelve thousand years ago, a sudden and more or less unexpected cataclysm caused the entire continent of Atlantis to sink and become submerged in less than twelve years. The eastern high points of Atlantis were all that remained above water when the cataclysm was ended and these mountain tops or mountain peaks now form the islands known as the Azores, the Canaries, Madeira and others. Even in Europe many great changes took place, such as the sinking of the ancient civilization of Athens and practically destroying all living Athenians. The continent of Lemuria had completely disappeared and only its rocky mountain eastern shore line remained and was now a definite part of the continent of North America. The inland sea that once existed between the Rocky Mountains and the Sierra Nevada Mountains in the Nevada basin, was now beginning to dry up and disappear, gradually reducing to a small sea. The present small Salt Lake of Utah is the last remnant of that great sea, and this is gradually disappearing. Some day, fifty thousand years from now, or even less, students of the history of the earth's surface will read with much doubt the story of the existence of a lake in the heart of Utah, just as many of you are reading with considerable doubt the facts regarding the inland seas of our present continents and the disappearance of continents of ancient times. There was also a small inland sea lying between the Coast Range and the Sierra Nevada Mountain range in California. This sea was in the northern part of California, lying in what is now the Santa Clara Valley and being a part of the present San Francisco Bay. Another small inland sea existed in the region of Puget Sound, for that was the northern extremity of the old land of Lemuria. In many parts of the present valley of Santa Clara, known for its very old soil and its wonderful relies of antiquity, sea shells of various kinds are found embedded in lands that are now high above sea level. Of other changes in Europe and other parts of the world we are not concerned in this book.

Lemuria had been torn to pieces and her great civilization submerged and lost, except so far as her colonies throughout the world were concerned. When the continent of Lemuria sank, it caused the water of the Pacific Ocean to recede on all coastlines and to change the shore-lines of all continents, leaving them higher and allowing many islands to appear that had not been visible before. When Atlantis sank the great hole left in the Ocean was immediately filled with an inrush of Ocean water which likewise changed the shore line of North America, allowing islands to be formed and some lands to be sliced off, such as a part of New York State being cut off and dropped into the Ocean forming the present Hudson River and the island of Manhattan, and that which is known as Long Island. The water of the St. Lawrence River and the Great Lakes and the Hudson Bay were drawn into the Atlantic Ocean at the same time, thus narrowing the rivers and making smaller the lakes and bays. We are not concerned, however, with the many changes that occurred throughout the rest of the world but with the results from the submergence of Lemuria, approximately twelve thousand years ago.

What became of her people? What races of mankind descended from this earliest race on earth? To what heights of civilization did she attain? What did she accomplish in her thousands of years of development and progress? Are there any remnants of her strange people living today? And what is the great mystery of California and the Pacific Coast of North America? These are the questions that interest thinking people today, and these are the questions that I will attempt to answer in the following pages.

THE LAND AND THE LIVING

*N*aturally, one of the first questions that is asked by every person who hears the story of the lost Continent of Lemuria is in regard to the land and the living thereon. What was the country like? How did the people live? And what did they do? The student of arcane literature invariably asks another question, "Did the Lemurians attain any special degree of intellectual, mental, or psychic development, as is sometimes reported?"

Regarding the nature of the country itself we have certain evidence from archaeological researches and undeniable testimonies in the form of relies. The country as a continent was probably not as mountainous as the western part of the United States except along the eastern shore, which is now a part of the State of California. The central part of the continent was more or less level with an occasional mountain peak rising to perhaps two to four thousand feet. These peaks were unquestionably formed through volcanic eruptions and undoubtedly the entire continent was badly shaken at times by the eruption of the many volcanoes which dotted every part of the continent. In the extreme western part of the continent there were some mountain ridges whose high peaks constitute the many islands near Asia.

The vegetation on the continent was undoubtedly of an extremely tropical nature. Viewing the continent from our present day considerations we would say that most of it was in the tropical zone but viewing it from the time of its existence we can say that all of it was of a tropical nature since most of it, if not all, was within an extremely warm belt. Those who have made a study of nature in its relation to the zones of temperature know that in tropical countries all living things of the vegetable kingdom grow to an extremely large size and in the animal kingdom all species lower than man in intellect and spiritual development tend to grow to extreme size. From specimens that have been discovered in various islands of the Pacific, long encrusted in the soil and preserved for us through many centuries, we see that even the smallest insects, as we judge them today, were of an enormous size in Lemuria. That which we call the ant today was so large that it was at least two inches in length in Lemuria, and the bug generally known as the roach, for instance, was from four to five inches in length, with large wings capable of flying a very long distance. All other animals grew to enormous size proportionately to those I have mentioned. The largest among the animals was that belonging to the class Dinosauria. These creatures grew to be over a hundred feet in length and sometimes much longer and they were undoubtedly the greatest destroyers of human life, animal life, and vegetation. Their strange grumbling, made by a form of gurgling in the throat, which always preceded one of their wild rampages in search of flesh, or the crackling of vegetation as their huge bulky forms moved through the high growth of grass and wild bushes, were sounds for which the natives constantly listened and in which they lived in dread.

Birds were especially prolific and of many varieties and it is believed by some of the best authorities that the eagles, especially that peculiar genus, the bald eagle found in the western part of North America is a remaining descendant of one of the huge birds that had its natural habitat in Lemuria, for it is found in some relics carved as an emblem, and in some pieces of stone parts of its wings, or the bony structure, has been embedded, giving us an excellent idea of its size and power.

Snakes and serpents of various kinds were also quite common and even though up to very modem times the belief in sea-serpents has been smiled upon by scientists who took the position that the sea-serpent was a mythical creature never having had real existence, it is now known that such creatures actually existed and that the ancient writings referring to them and the pictures carved by the Lemurians and their descendants were based upon actual facts. Only very recently, or within the year 1931, the first fairly complete skeleton of such a sea-serpent was found on American soil in the State of Texas where it was uncovered by excavators who had dug into virgin soil for the first time. Scientists who have examined the skeleton agree that the remains are many thousands of years old and that this gigantic Plesiosaurus flipped through the waters of the Pacific Ocean at the time that the Pacific Ocean reached inland to the district of Texas before the continent of North America was completely formed.

THE PLESIOSAURUS

From specially made photographs prepared for my study and examination I am convinced that the measurement of seventy-five feet for the length of the animal is correct. Its head is over eighteen inches wide and its neck over twenty-five feet long. Such creatures were evidently very frequently seen around the shores of Lemuria and were another source of terror to the inhabitants of the continent.

Perhaps the most interesting of the various species of animals that inhabited the continent of Lemuria and that which was the most prolific was that known as the *Lemurs* which constituted the class in the animal kingdom known as the Lemuroidea. Briefly and in non-technical language one may say that this class of creatures was much like that of the monkey or ape but with certain distinct differences which scientists have easily recognized even from the most fragmentary of specimens of skeletons. These creatures were of various sizes and in some parts of Lemuria, especially in the more tropical sections, grew to the size of the human body, or nearly six feet in height when standing up-right. With the average Lemur the tall was very long but other characteristics of well formed fingers and toes and well shaped heads have been responsible for an error being made in the judgment of those who found the earliest specimens of the skeleton remains of the Lemurs, and who thought that these fragments were parts of the skeletons of the humans who lived on Lemuria. This led to the conclusion that the Lemurians were an undeveloped sub-race of man. Many strange stories have appeared in various books regarding the native Lemurians and their primitive physical form and under-developed human characteristics.

The strange belief that man evolved from a continuous and progressive development of the Lemuroidea and that the eventual human Lemurian was a descendant of the ape-like Lemurs is also unfounded inasmuch as excavations and discoveries made within the past centuries have shown that the Lemurians as a race of man were highly developed in every physical and mental sense while the ape-like creatures were still true to their primitive form. There is nothing to indicate that the Lemurians were a primitive race except in the thousands, or perhaps millions, of years preceding the building up of the continent of Lemuria as a highly civilized nation, and there is no evidence that warrants the belief that the Lemurians were descendants from any lower specie of the animal kingdom. In fact this belief is abhorrent to every profound student of the Lemurian civilization.

It may be interesting to note in passing that the name of Lemuria as a name for the lost continent was arbitrarily adopted by scientists many years ago because of their knowledge regarding the existence of the Lemuroidea in the islands of the Pacific and the lands surrounding the Pacific and because it was believed that this class of creatures belonging to the primates had its original habitation on the continent that is now beneath the waters of the Pacific. The continent, however, is referred to in ancient writings as the motherland of Mu.

Regarding the people themselves, we have evidence that indicates that they were a little above the average of today, perhaps six feet in height and weighing around one hundred and sixty to two hundred pounds. They were of a strange appearance, however, with many unusual features. First of all they were not given to the eating of much meat, especially that of large or wild animals and when they indulged in flesh at all they ate that of small animals and fish. They lived principally upon vegetables and fruit and had discovered or evolved a method of baking many forms of food from vegetables made in the same way as our bread of today is made from wheat or corn. This method of eating had a considerable effect upon their manner of living, for, in the first place it did away with every invention or process for the hunting or capture of large animals or wild animals. This would naturally eliminate also the effects of hunting which have had a considerable influence upon the culture and modes of living of other races. Not being hunters they did not venture into wild parts of the country and did not become discoverers of new cities or new lands except as other forms of necessity might take them for short distances away from home sites or scientific exploration warranted. In fact new communities were established only as the old ones grew larger.

After the first great catastrophe that eliminated more than half of the original continent and left only a small continent in the center of the present Pacific Ocean the highest culture among the people of Lemuria developed along the eastern shore on the high mountain slopes facing the Pacific Ocean. Trade was exchanged between this shore and points of the new continent now known as South America. North America at this time was so swampy or covered with water that the raised parts, or those sufficiently above water to permit of habitations, were far to the south or north.

South America had afforded the opportunity for the establishment of cities and communities originated by those of Atlantis who had gone westward from the Yucatan in the time of their great catastrophe and there was a continuous exchange and communication between the Lemurian and the country of South America, especially the northern part.

While speaking of this exchange and trade it may be interesting to note one of the high developments and scientific achievements of the Lemurians. They did not use steam ships as we know them today although they did use the wind as one means of propelling or driving some of their vessels in certain directions. According to some carvings and writings found in very old records and buried specimens, they had found among the volcanic regions certain stones that had been thrown to the surface of the earth and which had a peculiar activity which affected water. When such a stone was placed in a large body of water it pushed or shoved water away from it in one direction with a very peculiar repulsion. This stone was used by attaching it to the rear part of a raft between two extended arm s so that the stone was held just slightly beneath the surface of the water. The stone was tum ed in such a manner that the repulsion of water was toward the rear. Since the water could not move away from the stone, the stone was forced forward and this pushed the raft in a forward direction. Whether there was any considerable speed to this mode of travel or not we cannot judge from our present day comparisons, but evidently it saved considerable labor and was sufficiently efficient to enable rafts and large enclosed vessels containing from ten to twenty men and a large store of supplies to make long journeys with safety. A form of steam propelling was known and used in many mechanical ways. Wind mills were also used in manufacturing purposes and there seems to have been another stone having some sort of magnetic repulsion, radiating an energy from it that was used to turn wheels that had large pieces of iron or some similar metal attached to its surface.

Light was also produced in homes or enclosures by means of some stone or mineral that was like unto radio-active ones discovered today, but which gave a very brilliant light continuously. Many rare minerals and unusual stones were used by the Lemurians in various purposes little understood by us since we have not yet discovered duplicates of them and from the occasional references to them, in writings or carvings, it is difficult to appreciate their nature and the purposes to which they were put. Evidently the continent in most parts was rich in minerals almost unknown to us today or else the Lemurians were so advanced in scientific knowledge that they were able to use many of the minerals now known to us for purposes unsuspected by us.

A large portion of the continent was constantly in a steaming condition due to the large areas of boiling lava. In this respect the surface of the continent in many places must have been like that seen near Naples with the hot boiling mud bubbling from the fires beneath and giving off steam continuously. I have walked among these beds of mud and studied the nature of the soil beneath and around such areas and have tried to picture the Lemurian continent with its active volcanoes beneath it and the other active ones rising high above the surface of the table lands, and it was easy to understand how such an continent might become destroyed and so shaken that the water of the Ocean would rush in over it and cause it to sink and disappear. Undoubtedly the large areas of boiling mud were lower than sea level and vegetation covered only those portions of the continent which were above sea level and along the shore of Oceans and rivers. This, however, would have permitted vegetation to have covered at least 75% of the continent.

Scientists have generally agreed in believing that the continent was four or five million years old at the time of its disappearance and this refers to the portion that remained in the Pacific after the first division and general floods which submerged the half of the continent lying east of Australia. Those scientists who have studied the evidence of the flora of Lemuria point out that it included principally coniferous and giant ferns while its fauna included many specimens of unusual scientific interest.

Whatever structures or buildings were erected by the Lemurians in the latter days of their civilization were unquestionably composed of stones of an extremely hard and durable nature much like granite and marble. Relies of these structures show not only the use of unusually hard stone but the use of a form of cement or mud for the joining of the stones and filling in of spaces between them that has stood the destructive forces of time, tide, and storm. The strange nature of the stone is one of the chief sources of evidence regarding the dispersement of the Lemurians before and after the great catastrophe. Structures have been unearthed in parts of South America bordering the Pacific Ocean, along the shores of Baja California and in certain parts of California and even in parts of Nevada, composed of this same hard stone, despite the fact that nowhere in the present excavations of North American soil have such stones been found in a natural state. This, along with the discovery of many unusual carvings, strange pieces of wood, specimens of unusual pottery and bead work and agricultural implements typical only of some of the Islands of the Pacific Ocean which are remnants of the lost Lemuria, give conclusive proof of the fact that the ancient Lemurians were in contact and communication with the shores of North America before the submergence of the continent.

The homes and other buildings were generally built in the form of rectangular walls averaging about ten to eleven feet in height over which wood and leaves and a coating of mud formed a roof. The roof extended from four to six feet beyond the walls on the outside thereby affording some shade around each building and keeping the interior cool. The extreme heat and the brilliancy of the sun was evidently one of the problems which the Lemurians had to contend with for there are many other indications that they suffered greatly from such sun heat on a continent where the very soil was warm from great fires and beds of lava beneath. There were numerous rivers and cooling streams due to the many small hills forming many valleys, which was most fortunate, and this, coupled with the fact that there were frequent heavy rains throughout the year, made it possible for the Lemurians to endure the heat and cultivate the soil. Larger structures were much like the small ones except in the height of the walls, and were composed of separated units with covered hall ways between them or perhaps long passage ways so that persons could go from one unit to another without going out into the heat of the sun. Other homes were carved into the sides of great rocks or mountains.

Most of the agricultural work, which was the principal employment of the populace, was done early in the morning or late in the afternoons because of the heat of the sun. Pottery and the making of ornaments seemed to be the chief manufacturing industry and this would indicate that there was a considerable exchange of these things between various sections of Lemuria and various other countries or continents. It is very possible that that part of Lemuria which disappeared first may have been considerably different in its soil and mineral elements and that there was a large exchange of the products of one part of the country with the products of another part sufficient to have warranted the Lemurians in the far eastern part devoting most of their time to the manufacture of articles of adornment, decoration, worship and mechanical service.

Wood was used to a great extent in the construction of buildings and in the manufacture of useful articles. The eucalyptus tree and the primitive form of the giant redwood tree were the principal ones to be found in Lemuria. The indications are that the eucalyptus was most prolific if not exclusively found in that part of Lemuria which was the first to submerge but a portion of which now constitutes the countries of Australia and New Zealand. However, young eucalyptus trees were transplanted in the far eastern parts of the continent and even brought to portions of the North American continent, and redwoods seemed to grow naturally along the eastern portion of the continent which now forms a part of the continent of North America. Thus we find in California the giant redwood trees acknowledged to be the oldest living things on the face of the earth, for some of these trees rising hundreds of feet into the sky are thousands of years old. But of this I will speak later.

Some very large buildings were built by the Lemurians undoubtedly as temples or places of worship and scientific study. Domes or curved roofs were quite frequent in connection with these larger structures and wherever a building was constructed for religious purposes the main entrance was a portal with the two crescent curves at the top symbolic of the sacred curve which was the basis of their religious-scientific doctrines.

There apparently was no attempt to build their homes close together or create congested communities although there was a very definite community life with definite precincts or districts for homes, temple buildings, and places of manufacture and agriculture. Streets and highways were formed by clearing away all vegetation and leveling a broad path and then covering this with a thick layer of powdered stone that was much like chalk stone in appearance but which when wet formed a hard united mass much like cement. In other places the wet, powdered, stone was merely sprinkled on the path and apparently no vegetation could grow through it and, therefore, such paths were kept definitely open and well defined. Transportation was principally by small boats on the many rivers for all the communities were located along the shores of rivers, but various animals were used to draw or pull what we might call sleighs, along the smooth highways while other creatures were used for individual riding. Many pictures crudely drawn show the native Lemurians riding on the backs of animals which appear to be tall and slender much like the camel, but of an entirely different form. As we shall see later on, there was not the need for personal contact and transportation in business and social matters that is common today and only those engaged in the transportation of merchandise or products of some kind felt it necessary to leave their communities and go to any great distance.

Gold and silver were plentiful as were other rare materials but these were used purely for ornamental purposes and not for exchange or any form of compensation.

All in all the Lemurians had a very difficult time because of the climate, the nature of the soil, and the continuous dread of unexpected volcanic eruptions, earthquakes, tidal waves, and attacks from hordes of wild creatures that would descend from the mountains or come from the plains or rise from the rivers and Ocean waters suddenly to at" tack a community. Despite all of these handicaps and difficulties, however, we find that the Lemurians achieved a great scientific comprehension of natural laws and at the same time developed inwardly certain human abilities to a degree much greater and higher than we have attained today, with all of our boasted advancement in civilization.

THE MENTAL AND PSYCHIC DEVELOPMENT OF THE LEMURIANS

*A*side from what we know of the descendants of the Lemurians and through a study of them discover the high degree of development achieved by their ancestors, there are many ancient records which refer to, and fairly accurately describe, the mental and spiritual development of the people at the time that Lemuria was in the height of its power. Ever must we keep in mind the fact that the civilization of Lemuria had developed through aeons of time. Europe may speak of its long periods of culture, and Rome and Athens may speak of the great heritage which was theirs, and even Egypt may boast of a long period of intellectual development, while we in America rejoice in the fact that there are some centuries of culture and development back of our present generation; but when Lemuria was in the height of her power she could boast of thousands of centuries of development.

In addition to the long period of time through which the Lemurians had learned the lessons of life and attained mastership through perseverance, industry, study and cooperation with the highest laws, they had the advantage of being free from the contaminating influence of false knowledge and a material conception of life.

Speaking in a purely spiritual and mystical sense we find that today those in Europe or the Western world who are seeking to comprehend the higher laws and principles of life deplore the fact that so much which we have learned in the past century or two must be unlearned in order that the intellectual consciousness of man may be cleared and purged and made ready to understand and inwardly comprehend the higher laws and principles. It is quite commonplace for students of these subjects to say that they wished they had come in contact with the real truths of life in their childhood when the mind was open, unbiased, and unprejudiced, and when the eyes had not seen so much through colored glasses and the ears had not heard so much through false trumpets. It is a fact that we are born with not only an inheritance of misunderstandings and false conceptions, but our environment and education from the hour of birth onward are fraught with the pressure and influence of false ideas and untruths. We struggle to separate the gross from the pure, to find truth amid so much falsehood, and to adjust ourselves to a correct understanding. Realize, then, what it meant to the Lemurians to have been free of this contaminating influence.

We admit that if a child born today, could be separated from the present influences of misconception and taken to a distant point and raised and trained in a purely natural spiritual way, with no contact other than that which is consistent with the understanding of higher laws, that such a child would become a great master so far as the highest principles of life are concerned. This was the situation with the Lemurians.

The Lemurians were not surrounded, right from the very earliest days, with any established conceptions of the universe or of the natural laws operating in the universe, and they had no established opinions or orthodox doctrines of life prescribed for them by any special group of scientists or educators, for all knowledge was obtained through the individual observation of Nature at work.

I do not mean to intimate that the Lemurians had no schools or institutions of scientific learning, for these are ample evidence to show that they did have these in abundance and operating with a system that would be most desirable today; but these institutions taught only that which was demonstrable, which had been proved true, and which the students could demonstrate to themselves. We find in all of the writings and records of the ancients that even thousands of years after Lemuria had attained its greatness in scientific learning and spiritual development the people had not fallen into the error of creating theoretical explanations and establishing hypothetical conditions to explain the phenomena of life. Our scientific schools today are filled with this sort of mental food and it constitutes one of the greater errors of our education.

The Lemurians and their descendants despised guess work and speculation in their learning. They came to realize that there was one dependable source of positive knowledge and this was the Cosmic Mind. It seemed to be common practice with them to resort to concentration and meditation when in doubt, or in search of new knowledge, just as we, today, turn almost automatically toward some printed book, the newspapers, or some specialist in human form, and accept the dictums, the principles, the theories, the ideas, the Personal conceptions and beliefs of these supposed authorities, without question. It is for this reason that in all of the later developments of their sacred literature, which constituted their real books of knowledge, they placed great emphasis upon the value of meditation and concentration, and we should not be surprised, therefore, to find that they became mighty and powerful in their ability to attune with the Cosmic Mind and in their further ability to comprehend, understand, and interpret the impressions they received. From these practices developed all of the sacred ritualistic practices of the various religions that developed among their tribes or descendants who went into other lands and established what later historians called the various religious rites and beliefs.

We may wonder whence came this great faith in the Cosmic Mind and the universal ability to receive information in this manner. Tracing back their own comments in this regard, we find that one very natural faculty which had developed in them was responsible for this great faith and trust in the Cosmic Mind. In order to make plain what this faculty was I must say something about the personal, physical, and mental, as well as spiritual, characteristics of the beings who constituted the Lemurian race.

If I could select a typical Lemurian, truly representative of those of his race who lived in Lemuria at the time of its greatest advancement in civilization, and place this individual before you as an exhibit, you would look upon a creature peculiar in many particulars. The first and most outstanding difference that you would notice between the typical Lemurian of ancient times and the typical man or woman of today, would be the fact that the head was very much larger in proportion to the body than we are accustomed to find, and we would notice that the forehead was very high, or that the distance between the eyebrows and the hair on the top of the head was much greater than in the average individual of today. In fact, the average forehead of the Lemurians must have been about six to seven inches in height. In the center of this forehead, about an inch and a half above the bridge of the nose, there was a large protrusion much like the size and shape of a walnut. We would look upon this sort of growth in the center of the forehead today, as a disfigurement, but with them it was perfectly natural, and such a protrusion was as proper to them as is the protrusion of our nose, or of the chin, or the high cheek bones. This protrusion, however, was composed of a soft mass of matter over which the outer cuticle was drawn tightly and the cuticle itself was of a delicate, soft nature and color like the skin that is underneath our eyes.

In height, these Lemurians were a little above the average of today, with a great many attaining a height of almost seven feet. The arms were much larger, longer, and well-developed in muscle, while the limbs were not so long but fairly well-developed. The hair on the top of the head was short, not through any style of dressing or training, and it grew very lightly and was of a very fine texture. The hair on the back of the head, however, grew very long, and was often braided or arranged in very fancy forms across the shoulders or down the back. If there was any one particular form of ornamentation it was in connection with dressing this long hair, and individual taste was given a wide scope in this regard, if we are to judge from pictures carved in stone or drawn or painted upon leather.

The necks supporting the heads were long and slender and usually a decorative collar formed of beads or stones was the only fancy addition to the adornment of the body. The feet and hands were large and every joint of the fingers and toes was easily moved and controlled, thereby developing them to a greater degree than we find in the present day races of man.

The women were somewhat shorter than the men and somewhat more corpulent, but their features were far more refined than those of the men. Very few of the men had any hair upon the face and the women protected their faces from the heat of the sun and from the effects of the weather by wearing a veil made of some vegetable fiber through which air passed freely, but the protection against sunburn was evidently sufficient to result in a fairer complexion for the women, throughout many generations, than was found among the men. The ears were much smaller than we find them today but the nostrils were largely developed and the nose was more broad and flattened on the face than we find among the people of the western world of the present period. The eyes were large and very clear, and gave an impression of a piercing gaze and keenness of perception that must have been very impressive. The skin was not of dark complexion but merely tanned, while the hair was very dark and the eyes were brown. The teeth were very small but uniformly even and regular.

The protrusion in the center of the forehead was a result of the sustained development of a faculty of the human body that has gradually disappeared since Lemuria submerged and the races of its people were dispersed throughout the world. I trust that my readers will not compare this protrusion of the forehead with the fantastic stories of Cyclops, but the story of Cyclops is based upon what was an actual fact with the people of Lemuria, for, although this protrusion in the forehead was not an organ of sight of a limited nature nor was it a "third eye" in a limited sense, it did constitute an organ of sense that was equivalent to an eye, and an ear, and a nose, and any other faculty that we now possess for the reception of impressions. It was commonplace for the Lemurian to close his two physical eyes and to stand still at any moment of his dally activities and focalize his consciousness upon the center of his forehead and receive an impression that might have been translated into one of sight or smell, or hearing, or feeling, or tasting. In fact, it was as common for the

Lemurians to suddenly turn their concentrated attention to this organ for some impression, as it is for us today to stop in our conversation or our activities, and concentrate our attention upon our hearing in order to hear some distant or faint sound, or concentrate our eyes upon something we wish to see clearly, or concentrate our sense of smell, or feeling, for a moment in order to analyze some impression. The Lemurian, however, used this special faculty not for local impressions or for purely intimate matters, but for long-distance impressions, for it is recorded that through the use of this faculty he could see or sense by smell or sound, some dangerous animal at a very great distance. In fact, he developed eventually, the ability to communicate with animals in their own language or their own manner of communication, through attuning this sixth sense with their own.

We should not be surprised to learn, therefore, that the art of mental telepathy or the mental exchange of ideas and impressions at unlimited distances became a perfectly natural, commonplace, and regular practice with the Lemurians. They recorded, in a casual manner, the reception of impressions from others who were hundreds of thousands of miles distant, just as a hunter today in recording his story of his hunting experiences would state in a casual manner that he heard the call of another hunter or the call of an animal five hundred or a thousand feet distant. To the Lemurians this sixth sense was not an extraordinary thing but quite commonplace, though they were conscious of the fact that its usefulness had been developed by their ancestors through practice and concentration and that it was a faculty more susceptible of development and growth than any of the other faculties which are common to the human race.

We, today, are conscious of the fact that our eyes can be trained in seeing, as witness the training given to an artist; or that our ears can be trained to hear, as is necessary with a musician; or our taste may be developed, as is true with those who are experts in the tasting of wine, for instance. We are likewise conscious of the fact that our muscles in any part of the body may be developed, or that certain features or functions of the body may be strengthened through definite effort and practice.

With the Lemurians the knowledge was handed down from generation to generation that the salvation of their race and the hope for mastership in the highest attainments of civilization depended upon the individual and personal development of this sixth sense. Naturally, they did not consider it a special gift and it is doubtful if they ever thought that the time would come in the development of the human race that that sense would become obliterated through lack of use and lack of development to such a degree that its existence would never even be suspected. They did believe and did understand that a lack of use of chis faculty in any family for several generations might result in a diminishing of its size or its high degree of usefulness, just as we realize that the discontinuance of the use of the tongue in speaking through several generations might naturally result in an offspring having no ability to use the tongue at all.

That this sixth sense was an organ equal to or in some way connected with the present small organ in our modem bodies known as the pituitary body is quite likely. And, scientists have discovered that in many of the races of man living today in remote parts of the world this organ is much larger than it is in those of more civilized races and that it has unquestionably diminished in size throughout the ages and must have been an important organ in some early races of mankind. However, that may be, this sixth sense also enabled these Lemurians to sense things in their *fourth* dimension, for one of the problems that confronts every student of their ancient carvings and writings is the continued description of things in a manner that shows that they saw or felt or sensed something about everything in nature of which we have no consciousness today. When they saw a tree, or an animal, a stone or a mountain, they saw more than its heighth and breadth and thickness. They saw something of a Cosmic nature or ethereal nature, to which they gave various terms; and to them it was as much of nature and as important in description as were the other three dimensions.

Now, if we add to this faculty and its abilities the further fact that it enabled them to attune with the Cosmic and to receive direct information of a dependable, reliable nature on all subjects and covering the entire field of knowledge, we will realize at once that the Lemurians must have attained an extraordinarily high degree of perfection, not only in knowledge but in the matter of living and co-operating with all of nature's laws.

Should we be surprised, then, that these people living on one continent, stretching almost half way across the globe, should have been intimately acquainted with the facts concerning the universe, the growth and development, rising and submerging of other lands, and other continents? Should we be surprised at their intimate knowledge of What was going on in distant points of the world far beyond their personal contact? And, should we be surprised that they had solved all of the great problems of life and had found solutions to all of the mysteries?

Their records and writings show that they were acquainted not only with the rest of the world as it existed during their time, but with what had existed on the face of the earth prior to the formation of their continent, and what would eventually happen to their continent. This was their guide in their wide colonization of other lands, and in the dispersion of their people to distant points in various periods. Again, we must take into consideration the fact that for over a hundred thousand years they had an opportunity of developing their knowledge and of carrying out their plans for preserving the race of mankind against the cataclysmic changes that they knew would take place.

To them the spiritual part of the world was the most important, because it was the only real part and the only dependable and safe part in life. Thousands of years of accumulated knowledge had taught them that the very foundation upon which they stood, composed as it was of earthly materials, and subject to the mighty changes that had taken place and would take place, was a most unreliable and unreal part of life.

Their conception of a future existence was quite unique and yet most logical, and probably as good as any that we have today. They were not only firm believers in the doctrine of reincarnation (not transmigration) but they had had ample time, and the faculty with which to prove, that reincarnation was a fact and that there were those living among them who had lived before on the same continent and in intimate contact with them. Therefore, reincarnation was not a matter of *belief* with them, for, as I have said above, they had no beliefs which were not demonstrable truths. They knew reincarnation to be a fact the same as we know that so-called *death* of the body is inevitable, and that the same body will not be seen on the earth plane again. This is not a belief with us but an established fact over which there can be no dispute. Their understanding of reincarnation was just as well established. But, they did know, also, that in the interim between the passing from this life and the re-embodiment of the personality again, the personality would exist in a spiritual world which they were not foolish enough to attempt to interpret in material terms like the clergy and the religious doctrinaires of today attempt to do.

They definitely stated that the personality of man was ethereal, spiritual, invisible essence and consciousness, which would occupy the fourth dimensional conditions of a purely spiritual world, and that such a world could not be located or described, limited, or compared with material terms relating to the material world. Even the Cosmic Mind which they looked upon as superior and above all human and material things, was not considered as being above them in a physical sense, nor located in the heavens or the clouds, as we think of Heaven today, but was considered to be in all space, everywhere, and for this reason they were apt to picture the Cosmic Mind or Cosmic consciousness as being within their rooms or even in the deeply excavated secret chambers beneath their homes, as in the vast space above the clouds.

For this reason the spiritual personality of one who had passed through transition was just as apt to be close to them and living with them in their homes or in their temples as above the clouds or anywhere else. That they could sense or contact these dis-incarnated personalities through their sixth sense is quite plainly indicated in their writings, but such contacts did not imply that such personalities were either close at hand or at a distant place inasmuch as this sixth sense received its impressions instantaneously, regardless of distance.

With such a nature and such an understanding of universal conditions it was only natural that the Lemurians should have developed a very high degree of appreciation of spiritual laws and principles.

Their conception of God was of a *universal principle,* both positive and negative, male and female, and Creative and loving in every sense. They had outgrown any earlier beliefs that their primitive forbears might have had that storms and strifes, cataclysms and destructive forces, were sent by gods of evil or by a loving God expressing His wrath. They looked upon all of the processes of Nature as constructive, even when temporarily destructive, and considered these as established laws of evolution having been created by a loving God in the beginning of time. Their interpretation of God as analogous to the human individual was much like comparing God with a *Great Master,* as well as *parent,* of all living beings. He regulated or controlled every process of nature with only one thought in mind, that of life and the perfection of the human race.

In another chapter I will speak of their communistic affairs, and their ethical and moral practices, for at present time I am speaking only of the individual as a highly spiritualised being. The refinement in the food they ate (being almost totally of a vegetable nature), the care which they exercised in what they drank, the manner in which they lived so far as hygienic conditions were concerned, coupled with labor, exercise, and rest, produced an unusually healthy body; but there was no attempt to seek a long life as the most desirable asset of the living. In fact, my readers may be surprised to know that they looked upon transition not only with a total absence of fear, but as a valued change and improvement in the status of the individual, and they were capable of deciding *when* transition should take place, and *how,* and it was common for the Lemurians at certain ages to announce to their relatives and friends that three days, or two days, hence they would pass through transition. They and their relatives would then make preparations for such an important event and all material affairs would be adjusted. On the day of the expected transition the devout ones would place themselves on that portion of sacred soil which they had selected to be their burial place, and with due ceremony lie down, bid farewell to all, close their eyes and go into eternal sleep within a few hours. Seldom were Lemurians stricken *unexpectedly* by any disease, and even accidents due to the attacks of savage animals, which was their greatest problem, were generally known to them in advance and every attempt was made to avoid such attacks. The average Lemurian, however, chose transition as the next step in his life after he became convinced that he had accomplished all that he could do or all that was expected of him in the conditions and circumstances in which he lived. For this reason, many Lemurians passed through transition in what we would call youthful ages, while most of them passed through transition between the sixtieth and seventieth year and a number out of every thousand lived to be over a hundred years of age.

If you, my reader, think that such a thing is impossible as the selecting of a day for transition and the arbitrary creation of such a condition without disease or pain or injury, you should know that there are still some groups or tribes living who practice this system at the present time, and the well-known explorer, Capt Salisbury has recently lectured upon his contact with transitions which he saw in various places. Many ancient records of the descendants of Lemuria show the continuance of this practice for many centuries after the continent submerged, and undoubtedly the pure Lemurian, or the pure descendants of ancient Lemurians who are still living in various parts of the world, carry on this same system as a quite natural solution to many of life's problems. It was not looked upon as a form of *suicide*, for in their ancient writings the willful ending of life by injury or undue risk of the maintenance of normal conditions in the body, is considered sinful, and any attempt to avoid obligations or the solution of life's problems by bringing life to an end was considered a violation of the highest laws. He or she who contemplated transition and prepared for it had to be able to show to relatives and friends that whatever their mission in life, it had been fulfilled, and that there were no uncompleted duties nor obligations, nor any fears from which they were Withdrawing in cowardice.

These facts will give you some idea of the Lemurian as an individual, and with these in mind we will make a little study of their community life and of their various moral and ethical codes.

THE SPIRITUALITY OF THE LEMURIANS

By Dr James W. Ward
(Eminent Disciple of Oriental Monastery Schools)

Some historians tell us that the Lemurian race was as unconscious of this physical world as we are in our sleep. To me it seems strange that historians having some facts about the Lemurians, will cover those facts with vague and indefinite ideas and statements which cannot possibly be true. In the next breath they admit the Lemurians were so spiritually developed that their consciousness was never concentrated on this physical world. They also vouchsafe the statement that their incarnations were a favorite pastime, laying aside the physical body when worn out and taking on another as naturally as the falling off of the leaves from trees and new ones coming out as beautiful as the ones cast off.

In the face of such contradictory statements they would have us believe the Lemurians were all born and lived without eyes, that they had no need of eyes, because, like animals and fishes in caves and underground, their eyes would atrophy from living in the dark. They go on and say that they had sensitive spots in their heads where the eyes should be and that the reflections of the sun affected those sensitive spots. First they saw they had no need for eyes and could not have eyes in a land of dense fog which the sun could not penetrate, and yet the burning glare of the sun caused great pain, and suffering to those sensitive spots in the head.

Such writings go on to say that the Lemurians never had a language, but they fall to explain how we got historical records almost as complete as that of George Washington. Writers of today say that the Lemurians were taught at the school of Initiation the laws of nature and facts relating to the physical universe, and art. Let me say at this time that the Lemurian of A rt was only used in reference to the Deity and, if I remember the wording of the old manuscript correctly, it was spelled *Ord*, translated ART . However, let us give thanks to those teachers for teaching a "blind" race which lived only in the spiritual and had no concept of the physical universe, yet were able to study the laws of nature and all the facts relating to the physical universe and art. Why not tell us where they, our writers, received their erudition? Where did they get their evidence that the Lemurians never had a personality nor an individuality, that they were only a God-guided people? I wonder how many of such writers have established and proved to themselves an individuality, and how I wish they had the divine apperception the Lemurians had. We must, however, thank them for stating that wisdom came to them as a gift. Personally, I wonder if God was not more generous in those days with His gifts than now? But why the argument? Let us establish the true facts and, unless I can prove to you that my friends have no ground to stand upon, you should refuse to accept my statements.

The first thing we were taught in the Oriental Monasteries, regarding the beginning of the human race called man, was that God was first, last, and always; that God was and is a supreme, divine, intelligence, who produced, evolved, and manifested man and every living thing. We were taught how and why man was produced. Our teachings were handed down from the Sages of Antiquity, and had been recorded in various ways and were perfectly understandable. They stated that God realized that every spiritual existence had to have a spiritualized manifestation in transition in order to be consciously conscious of its own existence, God having produced nature and every living thing had an idea of an ideal manifestation of the absolute, and He produced man as perfect as He Himself was perfect. If God failed in one millionth part of the perfection of man, and if our modem writers change that first man in any way, they destroy the existence of one Infinite God.

God's ideal in perfect man was a thousand times more perfect than I am today. I know that the Lemurian people were thousands of years old, the offspring of the original human family coming down through two long and interesting races whose earthly existence was purely immortal, that is, if the divine injunctions handed down from them to the Lemurians were authentic. That history was simply this: that man wanted to be free, he begged for freedom, he knew he was divinely free but he wanted to be a free moral agent; he knew more about liberty than some of us. God endowed man with reason and he lost track of his divinity; then came sickness, pain and death. Lameness and disease came into existence and from this there were millions blind, so many so, that thereafter the Atlanteans called them the blind race. However, there were many times more in numbers who were physically whole and pure as the angels in heaven.

Instead of pinning your faith on the lapel of our modem writers with their superficial knowledge, go with me and let us recognize the perfect man in all his innocence and purity. Their offspring for generations were proud of their ancestors who thought only pure, positive, constructive thoughts, and ever and anon endeavoring to emulate their forefathers and ancestral homes. They were constantly reminding their children of the Lemurian Disciples of God to whom they had vouchsafed the life and conduct of their posterity. Every night before retiring they taught their children to guard with care every action, deed and thought. To pray for strength and wisdom, to live the life taught them by the Holy Lemurians who lived in a world with other people, but not of them. True, they had love and compassion for the blind and diseased, but lived in a different sphere.

I, personally, viewed with interest some historical records of the Lemurians and especially interested was I in the fearless and undaunted adventures of twelve Lemurian Disciples who started out with an airship which looked just a little like our modem blimp. They were old men experienced in flying a ship, also in sailing boats. Their dreams were of exploring other countries or continents. They made some crude maps and some so plain and perfect that we were sure they were maps of Newfoundland and Florida.

These twelve Disciples finally landed in Atlantis where they were received, loved, honored and obeyed, because the Atlanteans called them the Holy Lemurians.

The records show that the Atlanteans knew all about the Lemurians and only referred to them as the blind race because of the great number of blind among them.

The twelve Disciples left a map of their travels, and it was of much interest to me because of the shape of the earth — almost round and resembling a coconut. The countries they discovered were sketched on the outside, similarly to the present day globe of the world. The Atlanteans in looking over the coconut shaped globe came to the conclusion that the home of the Lemurians was about a 30-day trip in a sail boat beyond the setting sun. To them the sun set just beyond the borderland of Atlantis.

I wish I had made a photo of that map as it looked to me. That was fifty-three years ago and I was not so much interested then as now. But there is now a very earnest desire on my part to reconcile the teachings of the Lemurians with the present day history and books, which teach that all was progression, that man at one time was of the lower animals. Some say that man actually walked on all-fours and that we still have the ape-body, etc. Sometimes I am inclined to believe it true of some writers.

Let us go over that old record showing the description, life, teachings, and mystical rites of the Lemurians, who were the most perfectly formed human beings that ever lived; straight as an Indian and as perfect a specimen of manhood as the Infinite Intelligence and the Eye of God could visualize; beautiful as a picture of a Greek God, and a soul as pure as the universal soul from whence it came and in whose image it was produced; as perfect as the Divine Mind could conceive; the highest idea of God produced for the sole purpose of manifesting God, demonstrating the good virtues and holy truths, so pure and sanctified that to observe one slight mistake or transgression of the law by a member of his family would cause him to hang his head in shame. Innately refined, the women were angels on earth; their grace and beauty excelled the most beautiful queen that has ever graced God's kingdom on earth. For 100,000 years they were as pure and as virtuous as the angels that are now on the Cosmic Plane. The pictures of those men and women showed them to be the color of the sun and equally as bright and shining. The men were nearer the color of the sun at dawn or at sunset while the women were lighter and brighter.

It is unfortunate to blur this picture with a history of those blind imbeciles and fallen angels that our modem writers would have us believe, completely inhabited God's own paradise. I am not going to comment on them for I might reflect some sad truths regarding our own modem civilized world. We still have a few men and women who are as pure and near perfect as is possible to live on this earth plane, while we have millions of old, dilapidated accumulations of ill spent lives traversing every stage of folly until we are getting millions of unclean specimens of humanity. Such degenerates of the Lemurian Race were in the minority, however great enough in number, and many of them lived in swamps similar to the swamps in Florida, before the country was drained. We have, today, in Sweden, cold, damp swamps, dark and dismal sections of country exactly like parts of Lemuria before the greatest upheavals and volcanic eruptions that were ever known destroyed the country and consumed the Lemurian race with the possible exception of a few. In truth and in fact they were not all lost and never will be, because the continuity of life came to their rescue and saved for them a remnant of the greatest, noblest race that ever lived. As a matter of proof of this narrative is the reincarnation of one of those twelve Holy Lemurian Disciples who was known in the Lemurian Age as the greatest architect that lived in that time and who has reincarnated many times, and each time for the love of humanity when man needed him most. He was born a perfect and pure soul, lived a spiritualized and perfect life through each incarnation. This Holy Lemurian whose incarnations have proven him one of God's noblest spirits is today doing God's work under divine guidance. He is dally designing and preparing those heavenly mansions and places of abode for all the elect who chose to *live the life* and become attuned to the "Threshold."

This short notation of the Lemurian Race is as true as the sun that shines and as perfectly narrated as the divine law that governs the divine plan of the universe.

THE COMMUNITY LIFE OF THE LEMURIANS

*A*ll the scientific analyses of the life of primitive man intimate that in the beginning of his earthly existence he lived separately and suspiciously isolated from others in the bows of trees or in caves along the banks of rivers until he learned whom he might trust among all the creatures of the animal kingdom. And we are told that he learned to trust a few animals of species lower than man and learned to trust a few of his companions and that eventually he domesticated the few animals he could trust and made friends of the men and women he could trust and these he gathered together in his immediate vicinity and constituted them as the elements of his community life.

Whether the Lemurians began their greatness in this manner or not we will probably never know. It must be evident to everyone who reads this book that the records from which we quote, including the carvings on many monuments and the traditions preserved in the writings of many races that descended from the Lemurians, began only with the story of Lemuria after community life was established. Men did not learn to think and analyze and had no occasion to preserve their thoughts and their knowledge until after they had learned to exchange ideas with others in the quiet hours of peaceful community life. Thus we find in the earliest records that community life was a well established condition among the Lemurians. When I speak of community life I do not mean the grouping together of individual homes, merely because of a favorable site or because of related conveniences that would bring a number of individuals and their homes together, for this was a stage that preceded the community life of which I speak. I refer to that form of community life wherein all the individuals in a group constituting a town site or a definite place of homes and dwellings were interested in some occupation, some production, some demonstration of mental and physical effort that made them live and work together as one large family. So united and identical were the interests of the individuals in most of these Lemurian communities that they appointed or elected one of their group who occupied a position much like a mayor, or city manager of today, but who was really their advisor, their chief instructor, and court of last appeal in all disputed points, and their religious and spiritual guide as well.

We may grasp a better understanding of the situation, perhaps, if we realize, first of all, that the Lemurians issued no coins and had no such commodity or device as money. No one received any form of remuneration for his efforts, except the privilege of sharing in all the community interests and each having the friendship and association and guidance of the principal minds in the group and of all the other workers. Their products were not sold and the things they made or grew in the soil of the earth, or which they dug from the mines, were traded with other communities at distant points where different products were available. Their storehouses and warehouses were community ones and there was no incentive to accumulate a vast amount of any of these products as a personal possession. The result of this condition was that each was required to give his very best effort in that direction for which he was best qualified and to that degree for which he was capable in exchange for the necessities of lire and the enjoyment of many luxuries and blessings which we do not enjoy today. The natural result of this is plain to be seen. Lawlessness and crime, as we understand it today, was reduced to a minimum. Social distinctions were absolutely without power. The power of personal wealth was unknown and probably could never have been comprehended by the Lemurians. Those who were talented in various ways were given every opportunity to exercise that talent and to devote themselves to it, for if it was productive in any sense it afforded an opportunity for receiving all of the blessings of community life equal to those who produced more material or necessary requirements. This is why the arts and sciences among the Lemurians progressed to a high degree. The reverse of this condition is true today. Eminent artists and scientists capable of making the most valuable contributions to our knowledge and to our ethical development are forced to abandon their work and their effort because they must resort to some occupation which pays them with money and enables them to live. If all of the truly great artists and scientists in the world today were assured of an equal degree and form of living and the enjoyment of all the necessities of life while pursuing their special professions, we would solve one of the great problems of the present and future development in our ethical culture.

I have already intimated that scientific knowledge constituted the religion of the Lemurians, inasmuch as a fundamental principle of their understanding was that God, or the Creator of all things, revealed to man all knowledge as a process of evolving man to the same degree of understanding as possessed by God. Therefore, the acquirement of knowledge was considered the acquirement of spiritual attunement, and growth and knowledge was looked upon reverentially, instead of as a commercial asset. That the knowledge should be applied in a practical way seemed natural to them, for otherwise there would be no purpose in the revelation of knowledge. Therefore, the religion of the Lemurians contained no doctrinal beliefs and no false gods or principles arbitrarily selected by any council or group of individuals and promulgated as an orthodox system.

In each community a temple of an appropriate size was built, handsome and enduring, as befitting a monument to the glory of its purpose and in which the religious services were of a double nature; namely, of silent or spoken adoration to God, with prayers of thankfulness and appreciation, and the dissemination of knowledge. These temples, therefore, were equivalent to universities and schools of the present day, and it is to be noted that the instruction was classified into various branches of study and presented progressively to the young people and in the form of forums and open discussions with those who had completed the youthful years of study. The education of the youth was compulsory, but the young people also had to contribute to their own support by participating in some of the practical work of dally life in accordance with their individual qualifications, talents, and capabilities.

It is from the records preserved in some of these temples and the carvings upon the walls of all of them that we have learned much about the Lemurians. These temples were typical of what the word temple means. They were buildings enshrined against time for the preservation of knowledge, as well as the giving of knowledge, and upon the walls of these structures, and especially on many large stones arranged in special position to stand the test of time, the outstanding discoveries and proved facts of life were carved for future reference. There are many indications in these writings that they anticipated the future to be very far distant and that much which they carved upon the stones would have to be preserved for many thousands of years in order that future races might learn the truth of these ancient people. We are sure, therefore, that these Lemurians anticipated some great cataclysm that might destroy most, if not all, of their continent, and scatter their people to all parts of the world and almost destroy all knowledge of them. It was this attempt on their part to prevent a complete obliteration of their existence that has resulted in our p resent day knowledge of them.

The moral standard of the Lemurians was extremely high, even though a modem purist would look upon their code as one of no morals at all, and would consider the Lemurians unmoral rather than moral or immoral. We find, for instance, a total lack of emblems or intimation that any form of phallic or sex worship entered into their consciousness. Our research would reveal that this phallic worship is a much later creation of uneducated men or races of men in distant lands. Among the Lemurians there was no prudery regarding the naked body, nor was there any particular reference to it for there seemed to be neither shame nor glorification of nudity, yet the

Lemurians did not dwell in nudity nor do they picture themselves as being undressed or lacking in dress in any degree. They wore loose flowing outer garments, much like the Egyptian and Arabs of today, which was probably as a protection against the sunlight and heat. But they had community swimming pools and bathing pavilions much like the Romans adopted in later centuries in which both sexes bathed at the same time without any consideration of sex or nudity.

There were very definite rules regarding all sex relations and they had a marriage custom that is still to be found among some of their descendants in some of the islands of the Pacific. According to records which have been found, the marriage system was as follows. When a young man and a young woman had found sufficient interest in each other to believe that they desired to become man and wife, they appeared before the official Gu of their community, who was their spiritual advisor, instructor, mayor, and Supreme Court judge. Their appeal was properly recorded and the relatives of both were called in consultation, and if the marriage was found agreeable to the parents a date was set for a ceremony that was preliminary to the actual marriage. On the day of this ceremony the young couple, their parents, and all in the community who were interested, gathered at the large open square or circle in front of the principal buildings and temple and the young couple were denuded of every bit of clothing and every worldly possession of a material nature. They were then escorted in a sort of fiesta parade with much music, flowers, and cheering, to the edge of the city or community bordering upon the wilds of unoccupied and unsettled land. They were then directed to proceed at least fifty miles inland into the wilderness in the company of each other, but without any material things, not even a piece of metal or device of any kind. In part of the ceremony the Gu or his representative suddenly demanded of the young man a piece of metal as a souvenir and token of his departure and the same was required of the young woman. If either of them possessed any thing of a materialistic nature or device of any kind the ceremony was postponed for a full moon period, or they were rebuked in some manner and not allowed to proceed. This test, therefore, was applied for the purpose of determining, in the presence of all witnesses, that neither one of the young people had anything concealed in their long flowing hair or braided locks or in their hands.

They were instructed to go into the wilderness and remain for a given time, usually two moon cycles or approximately two months, and then to return to the temple together and in the company of each other. If, upon their return, the young woman could show that she had some form of clothing, made from animal skins or from feathers and fiber, and had been well-protected against the attack of animals, properly fed and nourished and provided with comfortable sleeping facilities wherever they were in the wilds of nature, and, was convinced of the tenderness and devotion of the young man, and if he could show that he had provided himself with similar clothing and had secured proper food and protected himself against injuries and attacks from animals and could say that the young woman had been his help meet in every sense and that he was still fascinated by her charms and devoted to her, then a date was set for the marriage ceremony which was held in the temple with a very elaborate ritual, which included the making of an incision in the first or index finger of each of their right hands and the hands bandaged together so that the blood from one flowed into the other and thus became as one blood. The ceremony was a sacred one in many ways and constituted a form of marriage or union that was never to be broken except by transition. There was no such thing as divorce or temporary separation in the marriage relations of the Lemurians. If the young couple returned together or separately and either one claimed that the other had shown an inability to secure and provide food, sleeping accommodations, clothing, or was lacking in devotion or attention, the marriage ceremony could not be performed and the couple were never permitted to make a second application for marriage. In other words, the couple had to prove their individual abilities to care for each other, support each other, and continue to love each other under the most trying and difficult circumstances. We cannot help but wonder how many of the young men of today would be able to go into the wilderness without the least piece of material as an instrument or device and build a protective hut, make clothing, secure and prepare food, and care for another in similar circumstances. If such a test was applied today there would be few marriages, indeed.

All bartering and trading was done in accordance with certain standards and a violation of these standards disqualified the individual from sharing in any of the community interests for certain periods of time.

The young children of the community were cared for in a community nursery under the guidance of those who were specially selected to care for them physically, mentally, and even spiritually. Physicians were appointed in each community who developed a high degree of knowledge and skill in all systems of healing, including the use of herbs and surgery, and, according to some records found in different places, there was evidently a system of massage or exercise which was used as a part of the healing system for special conditions. Drugs or herbs were not depended upon exclusively, for a form of healing from the use of hands or the laying on of hands and another form of healing through meditation and prayer was in universal use.

I have already touched upon the subject of death, or transition, but we may add that no elaborate ceremonies or graveyards existed among the Lemurians, for after transition the body was considered of little importance. The mere fact that the average Lemurian voluntarily decreed his own time of transition, prepared his own grave, and laid himself into it and was willing to have his body become lifeless, indicates that little thought was given to the physical part of our beings. From some records we learn that three days after the transition had occurred, and it was found to be a true transition, the body was covered with some mineral or chemical much like lime, which ate away the body or destroyed every vestige of it without contaminating the soil. It is to be noted that in digging the grave the one who was to occupy it was always one of two who did the digging and the graves were always in lines running east and west and the head of the deceased was always placed toward the east. After the passage of many thousands of years there seemed to have come a change in regard to burial, for records show that the person who anticipated or decreed his transition did not lie in the grave but knelt or squatted in a position facing the east in a square excavation with his hands clasped in front of him and remained fixed in this position in meditation and concentration until transition came and some chemical was poured over the body three days later which made sure of the preservation of the flesh and bones against contaminating decay. Some graves have been discovered where the skeleton with some flesh is still in this kneeling posture with the dirt of the earth closed tightly around it. Since there were no individual possessions that were not owned by the community there was nothing willed or transferred to others at the time of transition except possibly some little ornament, or personal token, or keepsake, which never had any intrinsic value. Gold and platinum were quite plentiful but had no value except in the making of instruments and devices for ornamentation. There were few references to any minerals that could be considered precious, except a red stone which may have been the ruby, and if there were diamonds in Lemuria they were considered of no more value than pieces of glass would be. Rare feathers of a brilliant color were perhaps the most valued of rare ornaments known to the Lemurians and marble used in building some of the beautiful temples was the most unusual product taken from the soil and the most carefully used.

The homes were large and airy and sleeping arrangements consisted of a raised platform surrounded by a netting of fiber which afforded a protection against insects and small animals. This screen around each sleeping place was open at the top to allow ventilation. Food was cooked by fire or by the heat of the sun in special sun ovens. There were regular periods for daily worship and study for all members of each community and there were sacred features connected with the early morning ablutions just after sunrise, and again at sunset and at midday there was a community service of concentration and worship lasting for a few minutes.

This, in general, is a picture of the community life. It does not include, however, many of the vast activities of the Lemurians about which we shall learn in another chapter.

REMARKABLE ACHIEVEMENTS OF THE LEMURIANS

*A*side from the unusual psychic development or spiritual unfoldment attained by the Lemurians and which gave them unusual advantages in a purely personal and individual sense, the people as a race and as a nation attained a high degree of development in the arts and sciences and in the mastership of worldly problems.

When it is said in modem writings that the ancient Egyptians attained a degree of civilization and intellectual mastership that was superior to our present day attainments, this is generally said in a relative way, for it is only relatively true. When we say that the Lemurians reached a higher degree of civilization then we have reached, it is likewise meant in a relative sense, although there are some evidences of attainment that were actually beyond the scientific achievements of modem times.

When we stop to consider, however, the natural difficulties which surrounded these ancient peoples, and keep in mind the fact that they did not have the advantages which we now have and that many of our present day achievements are based upon discoveries which they made, we can truthfully say that these ancient peoples did attain a higher degree of civilization compared to the times and conditions in which they found themselves than we of the modern world have attained.

If a man is stranded in his youth on a barren island and during his lifetime is capable of evolving methods of extracting from the earth his necessities and turning gross matter into refined instruments and with these build beautiful homes and create the things he needs for a life of ease and luxury, we can truthfully say that he, as an individual, attained a greater degree of mastership in the arts and sciences than would an individual living during the same century in a modern city with all of the advantages and necessities supplied to him.

It is true that today we have many marvelous scientific achievements that are rapidly becoming commonplace, and which our children and grandchildren will look upon as ordinary conveniences of life. Many of these were undoubtedly unknown to the ancient people of Lemuria, or Egypt, or any other old country. To say, however, that these modern achievements, which we have and which they did not have, indicate a higher degree of advancement, a higher degree of civilization and culture than was enjoyed by the ancient people, might be a serious mistake. The Lemurians, for instance, did not have our modern radio methods, but even these modern methods of communication are becoming cumbersome and every scientist and philosopher dreams of further improvements whereby this cumbersome system may be simplified.

We may find, for instance, that the methods which the Lemurians had for communicating to great distances was a higher phase of scientific achievement than our present day radio, for I have already explained to you that the Lemurians were capable for mental communication, regardless of distance, through the effort of a faculty which we have dubbed "mental telepathy." This would indicate that whereas we have placed our faith in the forces of nature, such as electricity, and have created machinery for the transmission of this energy from one distant place to another, the Lemurians proceeded along much higher lines and developed a faculty within their own beings for the transmission of an energy more refined and higher in its vibrations than the crude electrical energy which we use. Their means for distant communications was not surrounded by cumbersome equipment and by interferences from electrical storms and by rules and regulations and by finances. The ease with which they could communicate and the dependability with which the communications were transmitted and received certainly represents a higher achievement in this field than our present day radio, just as radio and telegraphy represent a higher achievement in our art of communication.

In many Oriental lands, today, tourists of the thinking class and investigators are frequently astonished at the rapidity with which a story or a message or an important fact is made known to various persons at very distant points. The art of communicating thoughts is still a mysterious art, despite all of our scientific achievement, and is really classified among the arcane mysteries awaiting further scientific development.

In many other respects, however, the Lemurians achieved great fame and mastership. In the art of building, for instance, the Lemurians constructed with plans for greater permanency than any other nation of people. They knew from long experience that their continent, as well as the rest of the world, would be rocked and shaken by earthquakes and volcanic eruptions and that periodic changes in climate would also affect everything that they built. They, therefore, made a careful study of the science of balancing and the art of calculating the principles of stress and strain. When we realize that some of their structures stood for nearly thirty thousand years without being damaged by any of the cataclysmic changes, we see at once how marvelously they had mastered this problem. When we think of how modem built buildings, designed and constructed by architects and contractors who have access to all the facts and figures of the earth's changes, are quickly thrown down by even light earthquakes or temblors, we cannot feel such great pride in our achievements in the art of building.

As we pass by any modem electric or steam power plant and see the enormous amount of material, labor, and money invested in such elaborate equipment solely for the purpose of giving us a form of nature's energy, and then think that the Lemurians used the natural energy without all of this equipment, we see that we have not progressed as greatly in our mastership of the earth as we think we have.

The Lemurians harnessed all of nature's forces in a truly scientific manner and with extreme efficiency. I have spoken of how they were able to propel their boats in water by using the energy that radiated from a stone. Undoubtedly a similar device was used in the propelling of their airships through the air, for they did use air-ships quite frequently. Since they needed no engine, no gasoline, and no long-armed propellers,, their airships were lighter and much different in design from anything that we have been able to attain at the present time. Furthermore, they were able to have lights in these air-ships and to use a searchlight that cast a beam to a greater distance than is cast by any of our present search-lights. Whatever the nature of this light, its energy was not produced by any revolving machinery or by gasoline or gas, but undoubtedly from some minerals small in size but which could be so harnessed or utilized that their radiations furnished the necessary energy.

We are only beginning to study the nature of radio-active or radiating minerals and we are only speculating at the present time on the possibility of harnessing our natural, universal energies. Scientists tell us that there is sufficient stored-up energy in one atom to cause A terrific explosion, if we only knew how to use this energy and apply it safely. The Lemurians, either by force of circumstances or through a greater understanding of Cosmic energies, were able to use the power in many minerals and apply this power very specifically and efficiently. One of the outstanding features of Lemurian scientific achievements was the utilizing of the energy and power that is constantly bathing this earth in the sunlight. In our present day period of scientific achievement, we are just speculating with this possibility and a few small engines have been constructed which operate with sun power. The Lemurians used this sun power very freely and very universally in all of their communities. It gave them light and heat and energy at night and gave them enormous motive power during the day for the movement of great pieces of stone and wood in their constructive operations.

In botany they were so expert that agriculture with them became like the expert work that is shown at a botanical garden. In art they were guided by their superior knowledge of fundamental Cosmic laws and by certain rules which are taught today only in the architectural schools, but which they used not only as fundamental principles for living, but in all of the sciences and activities of earthly life.

Many of their homes were carved in solid rocks on mountain sides; on the other hand, others were built of rare stone to represent in symbolical form the great temples of knowledge having spiritual or Cosmic lines and contours.

These Cosmic principles were expressed in many ways by the Lemurians but we find the fundamental law of these principles expressed by the Lemurians as "The Law of the Sacred Four."

The drawing given herewith illustrates some of the forms in which The Law of the Sacred Four was represented either in a very definite form, like the plain cross, or in a decorative form. It will be noticed that generally a circle was drawn around the outside of the symbol of the Four since this circle represented the lines of the universe and carried the intimation that the completed universe or anything in its completed expression, having no beginning and no ending and lasting eternally, was based upon the Law of the Sacred Four. The center example at the bottom of the drawing shown herewith, containing a cross with its sides touching the circle, became known in later years among the descendants of the Lemurians as the Wheeled Cross. While it is true that this form also became typical of the wheels found on the earliest carts or wagons, the *wheel* was connected with this symbol because of the turning of the earth and the passage of earth through Cosmic space. In other words, it represented revolution. This Wheeled Cross later became the first symbol of the mystic Rosicrucians who were the inheritors of the earliest mystical teachings of the Lemurians through the mystery schools of India and Egypt.

SYMBOLS OF THE SACRED FOUR

The four principles referred to by the Lemurians in their legend were the Creative principles of the universe, as well as the four fundamental laws governing the geometrical and mathematical form of everything that was created. Since the outside circle represented the universe, it was sometimes drawn in the shape of an egg, for the Lemurians considered the egg as symbolical of the birth place of all living things. The Sign of the Four, showing the cross within the egg, represented the process of germination. An ancient Lemurian legend said that in the beginning God commanded the four principles to bring forth all life and that the four principles began their work within a Cosmic egg. It may be interesting to speculate for a moment upon the many forms in which the cross has been adopted as a symbol by various races of persons in all ages of time and even as a symbol of religious and philosophical thought. This is just another in stance of how A truly sacred or spiritual and philosophical principle, universally recognized today, can be traced to the high spiritual illumination of the Lemurians. The designs shown herewith are drawn from many ancient Lemurian carvings, found not only in California and South American communities established by the descendants of the Lemurians, but on many of the islands of the Pacific.

The Lemurians must have enjoyed life to the fullest extent, for they had invented and devised ways and means of producing all of the necessities and all of the luxuries required by them. Certainly, the present day races of man have not reached this point. We have entered into a cycle of artificialities, bringing forth artificial and unreal desires that can be satisfied only with artificial things. We have developed the stage and the production of theatricals as an artificial means for the study of history and human problems. Having entered into this fictitious manner of study, the stage has rapidly developed until we believe the theater plays and moving pictures are of educational value and Areal necessity as a form of amusement. If we can realize for a moment that the real study of human beings around us and an analysis of things that are actually occurring in every-day life are the basis of all theatrical productions and could easily supplant the artificial productions on stage or screen, we will see that the Lemurians missed nothing of the luxuries of life through not having our present day moving pictures, despite the fact that we consider any community in which there was no theater or no pictures of this kind as being antiquated and lacking an essential form of pleasure.

The same principle is true regarding many of our other modem accomplishments. The seeming necessity for money and the seeming necessity to save time are two of the artificial standards responsible for most of our modem scientific achievements. We require automobiles and other means to transport us rapidly from place to place in order to eliminate a false valuation of time. Our radio is an attempt to out-do the telegraph and telephone, as well as the post in the transmission and reception of communications, but here again it was the element of time that was given the greatest consideration. We are building great buildings and great communities, not because of the artistic arrangement but because of an artificial necessity based upon an artificial valuation of land.

If we analyze what we have today as representing our advancement in civilization, we will find that we have gained nothing that the ancients did not have and which they enjoyed to a greater extent because of its naturalness. Of the artificial things, however, or the unnecessary things brought into existence by a false realization of life itself, we will discover that most of these could be eliminated from our life if we lived properly, and their lack would not constitute Areal detriment nor an obstacle in the attainment of peace and happiness.

The Lemurians, therefore, devoted themselves very greatly to the establishment of communities in distant lands and to the education and advancement of the races of man which were emerging from the early foundations laid by their own people. In one old record there was found an interesting story of how the later descendants of Lemuria visited a community in Alaska which had been founded by some of the early pilgrims from Lemuria. These late voyagers expected to find these descendants in Alaska enjoying all the advantages of life which the Lemurians had created on their own continent. They were surprised to find that these people in Alaska had retrograded and had become so distinct in color of complexion, in manner of dress, in form and habit, and even in writing and speaking, that they had difficulty in becoming convinced that they had not come upon an entirely new race of earthly people. Great missionary work was attempted to aid these descendants in modernizing their communities and reaching the same degree of development as those who had remained on the continent of Lemuria. It appears, however, that they never completely succeeded in doing this and abandoned the work because they found that the climate and general conditions had made the people lazy and indifferent in cultural development, and it is more than likely that from this period onward through history, this tribe in Alaska spread into other lands, intermarried, lost most of its racial distinctions, and became a nomadic people probably still remaining in northern zones.

The pilgrimages to other lands were highly successful and records show that the Lemurians kept in contact with their people in Mexico and South American countries, and in Egypt, Asia, and parts of Europe, throughout many centuries, and through this continued contact and comparison of ideas and principles there came to be a universal establishment and agreement in regard to certain points of agriculture, buildings, language, music, art, ritual, and other human activities which are outstanding points of racial identification today.

THE COLONIES AND DESCENDANTS OF THE LEMURIANS

*C*onsidering that the Lemurians were the first definite races of man known to history and that the continent of Lemuria was the real cradle of the civilization of man, we are confronted with the interesting fact that from Lemuria and its people came all of the present day races of man.

The fact, however, that Lemuria was a very large continent, reaching more than half way around the world, answers one of the interesting questions about the great variation of races and tribes of people found in even the earliest periods of research. As has been stated in a previous part of this book, climate and environment and the desires or exigencies of life are responsible for most, if not all, of the variations we find in the complexion, build, countenance, features, customs, and habits of all of the races of man. Man, as God created him in the original divine image, was of one definite type, and if all external influences had never affected this type, the descendants of the first man and woman would have been of a similar nature, except for the changes of evolution resulting from inner growth and spiritual development.

Considering, however, the enormous size and expanse of the continent of Lemuria which brought its habitable portion into various climates with a great variation of soil and the products of the soil, and considering the great age of the continent and its people, which included many cycles of cataclysmic changes not only in the material nature of the continent itself but in its climate and in the effects of these things upon the people, we can easily understand how the race of Lemurians, as it spread throughout its own continent, through many centuries, developed tribes of people with varying complexion, varying forms or degrees of development of forms, and greatly varying habits and customs.

Unquestionably, in the early periods of Lemurian civilization pilgrimages were made quite frequently in search of the fortunes of life and the satisfaction of the natural curiosity of the intellect for worldly research. Many of these pilgrimages must have been made to very distant points of the continent and at these distant points colonies of communities were established and maintained. The wide separation of these and the distinct differences of climate, soil, and the requirements of life gradually brought about many changes in the figure and personality of the members of each of these groups of colonies or communities, and in each case a foundation was laid for the beginning of a new tribe or a new branch race of the Lemurian people.

There were parts of the Lemurian continent that were extremely cold and undoubtedly passed through the serious effects of the so-called Glacial Period. There were other large areas of the continent that were within the belt of the most extreme tropical weather. When part of the continent was experiencing the colds and storms of winter another part of it was in mid-summer. These are but a few of the outstanding facts that must be taken into consideration in trying to form a mental picture of the growth and development of the various tribes or races of man that descended from the early Lemurians.

Many of their pilgrimages made to distant points resulted in complete isolation and permanent separation from the original race. Time is a tremendous factor not only in the development of human characteristics but in the gradual blotting from the memory most of the past traditions, customs, and habits. Many of the colonies or communities established by the expeditions of Lemuria eventually lost all trace and record of their earlier connections and developed even a distinctly different tongue and manner of living, adapting themselves to the conditions in which they found themselves and adapting themselves to the gradual changes that took place in the course of a hundred thousand years.

It is natural, however, that certain elements, certain principles, certain beliefs, or traditional facts, should have remained vague and indefinitely fixed in their consciousness, and that is the one due found in the search of the races of man which enable us to relate them to a common origin. In those things which were recorded more or less permanently by the earliest members of the Lemurian race there were fixed ideas which were carried forward through thousands of generations. When knowledge is conveyed mostly by word of mouth from father to son, and generation to generation, we expect to find continuous modifications, amplifications, and distortions, as well as unexpected elaborations, but in those matters of greatest concern, which were cut or carved into stone and which remained permanently visible and fixed for thousands of years, we find the permanent similarities and universal agreement in certain ideas which help us to unite one race, one tribe, one people, in various parts of the world with others.

Those things which are considered the most sacred to the individual are the ones which are most apt to become permanently fixed from generation to generation. Among such things are definite holidays or holy days, certain community practices or customs, and certain ideals. As I have already stated in another part of this book, we find, for instance, among the many and greatly diversified tribes of American Indians on the continent of North America and even in South America, certain holidays, certain ideals, certain words, and certain customs which are uniform and universal among all of these diversified tribes of people, and we find similar holidays, customs, ideals, and habits among races of people living in isolated parts of the world who are not physically or mentally classified as being connected with or a part of the Indian tribes. We cannot avoid the conclusion that all of these peoples with such similar and unique agreements in certain points must have had either a common origin or a close companionship and connection at some distant time.

We know, furthermore, from the records that have been preserved, that as the western part of Lemuria, located in the Indian Ocean, began to suffer from the cataclysmic changes and to sink beneath the surface of the Ocean, that the people of Lemuria began to disperse themselves in various directions. Africa was the closest land to this western portion and, in fact, a part of Africa as we know it today was at one time a part of Lemuria itself. But the portion of Africa that overlapped Lemuria or touched its shores in other parts was a vast swamp-land at the time that Lemuria began to submerge and except for a few high parts which eventually became mountains and now constitute islands in the Indian Ocean, the most habitable lands to which the Lemurians could go during the periods of their catastrophe were toward the east, including those high parts that now constitute the islands of Sumatra, Java, Borneo, New Guiana, Australia, New Zealand, and others.

As the continent continued to become submerged those who had located more or less permanently on the above mentioned places found that these were remaining high and dry and safe for habitation and did not continue their eastern pilgrimage but stayed where they were and became founders of new countries and eventually of new races of people.

In later centuries, however, the colonizations and pilgrimages spread to the shores of South America, North America, and through the continent of Atlantis to Africa, which had emerged from its swampy grave and was now a habitable continent. Those who ventured to such distant points found in succeeding years that they were separated by vast expanses of water from their original country and, adapting themselves to local conditions, became founders of other races of man.

I have already explained how the climate and sunlight in vast open areas would tend to darken the skin of some races of people, while those living in colder or in moderate climate with much more vegetation, or in the forest, would have a lighter complexion. The other shades of complexion which are often erroneously used as guides to distinguish races of man, are likewise effects of climate and environment.

If we skip a hundred thousand years or more and take up our study of the races of man at practically two thousand years before the Christian era, we find the races of man widely distributed throughout the world with accumulated and firmly fixed distinctions which were so at variance that if one were to judge them as we would have found them at this time, without any regard for their past associations, we would have to conclude that most of them represented independent races that never had a common origin.

For instance, in the year 2000 B.C., we find eight very definite classifications of peoples which may be called the Aegeans, Egyptians, Hittites, Amorites, Iranians, Indians, Huns, and the Chinese. The latter six constituted the general groups of Alpine, Proto-Nordic, Semitic, Mongolian peoples, while the first two classifications represented the Mediterranean people.

We find that the Aegeans at this time were the sea going Cretans of the first Middle Minoan period who had developed culture under Egyptian influence and built a monumental city at Cnossus, which became the political and commercial capital for trading with Egypt and Babylonia. They evidently became the leading sea power of the Mediterranean and made rapid advancement in civilization, even though their country was destroyed several times. They became competitors with the Egyptians in the development of architecture and art and established colonies in Sicily, South Italy, and Asia Minor. They were finally in conflict with the Greeks and from their contact with these people a new branch race started to develop. The Aegeans entered into Syria and some of their people became the Philistines mentioned in the Bible. From this time, which was about the thirteenth century, B.C., the pure race of Aegeans became mixed with others and in a few hundred years was almost extinct as one of the ancient original tribes, while the Greeks descended from them and developed a new culture and civilization which increased in power throughout the pre-Christian centuries until it began to diminish about the second century after the Christian era.

The Egyptians constituted one of the branches descending from the early colonizations of the Nile soon after the submergence of Lemuria and in the year 2000 B.C., had developed agriculture, shipbuilding, government, commerce, art, law, writing, and mathematics. Thus, we find the Middle Egyptian period of the 12th dynasty, a time of reunification of Egypt into a strong feudal State under Theban Kings. A century later Egyptian culture was at its zenith and considered the most perfect in the world. The worship of the sun as the god Ra was first established in this country during the 19th century, B.C., but Egypt was then beginning to pass through a period of internal strife and disorder. The situation was saved by the introduction of new blood through the invasion of the Semitic Nomads or Bedouins who ruled over Egypt as the Hyksos Kings. It is interesting to note that about this time hordes were introduced in Egypt for military purposes and this military development became so extensive that it actually laid the foundation for our present-day military rules and regulations and the carrying on of wars in a systematic and supposedly semi-humanitarian manner. A rt suffered as a consequence although the political power had increased to an extent that the resulting wealth and authority produced many marvels of architecture. Finally the Hyksos were expelled with the aid of an army raised in Ethiopia, where an early group had colonized and a dark skin race had developed. The introduction of this blood into the Egyptian valley had a very definite effect upon the future generations.

About 1500 B.C., the Egyptians entered into trade and commerce with Babylonia, and there was a sudden development in literary activities producing many of the famous sacred writings now familiar to us, including the "Book of the Dead." Soon, thereafter, a great statesman, Thutmose III, who has often been called the "Egyptian Napoleon," conquered Syria and Ethiopia, and Thebes, the capital of Egypt, rose to the height of its greatest splendor under the marvelous intellect and power of Queen Hatshepsut. This was the beginning of the rise of the Egyptian empire, and from thence on the magnificent temples at Karnak and Luxor and elsewhere were built, and art and the sciences were at their height; but this power was bringing in its wake a definite moral decline which eventually threatened the prosperity of the empire.

The descendants of Thutmose III and Queen Hatshepsut realized that religion, morals, and ethical culture were required to save the empire and the races of man, and in the 14th century B.C., the members of the royal family made their first plans for a system of cultural development and for the organization of secret schools and institutions for the spread of such knowledge. The plans culminated in the birth of one unique king, Amenhotep IV, who not only changed his name to Ikhnaton or Akhnaton, but changed the religion, the art, and all of the scientific, political, and ethical foundations of the country. In religion he introduced the idea of a "one ever-living God," existing above and beyond all the symbols and all the terms for any god, and greater than any of the past gods or any of the living creatures on the face of the earth. This was the first introduction in the modern world of the ancient Lemurian idea of a monotheistic religion. His ideals, however, were criticized and attacked by the pagan priesthoods and he and his followers had to resort to the establishment of secret mystery schools and fraternities for the continuance of their religion, and the furtherance of their moral and ethical codes. In these plans, successfully carried out, we find the foundation of the first secret fraternities with secret initiations, pass words, and means of identification, which later developed into various forms of guilds, crafts, and fraternal lodges.

Amenhotep IV died without a son to succeed him, but he had seven daughters, one of whom became queen in her childhood and who married a scheming politician, by name *Tut-ankh-amon*. This youth attempted to convert the wealth, the art, and power of Egypt to his personal aggrandizement through making peace with the pagan priesthood and converting the official religions and morals of Egypt into the lower standards of the priesthood. His transition occurred while he was still a young man and he was buried in a structure created by him as a hiding place for the wealth he had pilfered and accumulated, and this great tomb was discovered in recent years.

From his time on the power of Egypt waned, and after the 12th century B.C., there was a rapid decline and Egypt was attacked by the Lybians and others, and the final dissolution of the great Egyptian empire occurred in the 11th century B.C. It was just before the fall of the empire that tribes from other lands invaded Egypt and became the tribes of Israelites that later left this land and went into Palestine, Syria, and other parts of the world.

The Hittites were really descendants of Indo-European races who had inter-married with the Alpine races and became the ancestors of the present Armenians. In the year 1800 B.C., they had established a kingdom in Anatolia and developed the peculiar writing known as the cuneiform, as an adaption of the pictorial representation of the Indo-European language. They developed their religion in which they worshiped the great earth as the mother of all living creatures, and their history after the 17th century B.C., is little known. They built many imposing palaces in later years and their king, Hattusil I, expanded their territory into Syria establishing the Hittite Empire. They became politically united with a formidable Iranian power in the east and attained the height of their glory in art and civilization in the 14th century, B.C.

About the time of the exodus of the Israelites from Egypt the Hittite kingdom began to weaken and later on through the invasion of the Assyrians their language was changed, their customs and their habits, and the Hittite Empire faded out of the world picture in the 9th century, B.C., while the Syrians as a distinct race succeeded and evolved from them only to fade out as another world empire in about the 8th century B.C., although their people blended with others and the Syrian ideals and customs and habits continued for many centuries.

The Amorites were perhaps the most spiritual and artistic of all of the tribes or races descending from the Lemurians and they gave most of their thought to the formulation of codes of law and to the development of art and literature. At about the year 2000 B.C., they were beginning to establish the great Babylonian kingdom with the wonderful city of Ur where culture was developed to that of the highest degree in any part of the world. In fact, the word culture itself is derived from words meaning, "the Light of the City of Ur." The city of Chaldea succeeded Ur as a great center and the people absorbed the Sumerians and other tribes until we find a new race evolving which established the Kasshite dynasty. Their art and culture, however, began to decline in the 17th century B.C., and they developed a religion worshiping the moon as a god with a great temple dedicated to this god built at Ur. The Kasshite power began to decline after the 16th century B.C., and at the time of the entrance of the Israelites into Palestine and Syria the Babylonia-Amorite power was rapidly decreasing. Finally an evolved race, descending from them, established the Babylonian power about the 10th century B.C. From these descended the Chaldeans as a ruling caste and a controlling power among their people, and after they had attained the height of their splendor in the 6th century B.C., the Chaldean empire gradually faded out until at the time of the 4th century B.C., it was of no consequence, politically or socially.

The Iranians in the year 2000 were composed of groups descending from the early Elamites, Mitani, Cossaci, and the Aryan Hindus. They probably brought the first horses to Asia Minor and Mesopotamia and records show that they were the first in Asia to use the Lemurian bows and arrows as weapons. They were experts in the making of finely painted pottery, and 1800 years before the Christian era, had perfected a pottery wheel that greatly advanced the manufacture of pottery. The centers of their art and culture were located at Susa (Elam) and Anau. The coming of an increased number of Elamites into India in search of gold and copper increased the power of the Iranian Empire and they became famous for well-built palaces and buildings, and for the introduction of unique drainage systems into their communities. The race of Iranians continued to remain strong and definite in character and the power of one of their kings, who destroyed Babylonia and carried away much of its wealth, might have been the beginning of a great empire, but it was, in fact, the beginning of a decreasing and diminishing empire until the coming of that great prophet, Zoroaster, in the 9th century B.C.

His new form of the monotheistic religion of the ancient Lemurians and a revival of the culture and ethics of the people of Lemuria gave his people new life and new power. A great mystical religion and philosophy developed among their people who later became known as Magians. In the 6th century B.C., Cyrus established the Persian empire which included the Iranian races and finally included the peoples of other countries. It was during this period that Zoroaster's great work entitled "Avesta" was compiled and the Persian empire was born.

Warfare had spread to the seas and the Persian empire defeated the Greeks, but a decline of Persian power followed this great victory even though the culture and philosophy of Persia was at its height. There followed centuries of crime and disorder until their king, Darius III, was defeated and their culture and power were absorbed by the Hellenistic conquerors in the second century B.C. From their people, however, descended many other tribes and races, and once again a new Persian empire came into power for a short time between the 2nd and the 8th century, A. D.

The Indians, or Hindus, constituting perhaps the purest blood of the Lemurians and known as the pure line of Aryan speaking people, were found in a more or less primitive State in India at 2000 B.C., because of their world-wide pilgrimages before having established a group of permanent communities. They finally invaded the Punjab, which had been inhabited by a race that had become so dark in complexion as to be considered the foundation of the black races of man, and in this country the early Indians established the tribal system of government and developed agriculture to a high degree. The Elamites were also absorbed partly into the Indian line and this had a powerful effect upon the religion and art of the Lemurians. Their literature developed to a very high degree and in the 15th century B.C., they began the compilation of over one thousand poems describing their life, early ancestry, and their religion. These were grouped together under the general title of "Rig-Veda." Sanskrit became the national language thereafter and because of the great literary and art learning among the better class of their people there was developed a Hindu or Indian caste system. In architecture they developed the method of excavating into the rocks and in the mountain sides and building cliff temples. This feature of their civilization reached a magnificent degree in the 11th century B.C.

Finally their priests obtained supremacy over the nobles and political rulers and there was an increase in their territorial states and associated kingdoms. At about the time that Zoroaster appeared among the Iranians with his revelations of ancient religions there was developed among the Hindus and Indians the Brahman system of religion.

It is interesting to know that in this same century the Babylonians developed a new form of spiritual understanding and in Assyria new temples and edifices were erected to a more human god. In Palestine, Judah, and Syria the Jews were evolving a new religion with Solomon building a great temple in which the religion was revealed. The Phoenicians had developed in that same century a new alphabet for the purpose of recording their religious ideals, and from this came the alphabets of all the western civilization. At the same time in Abyssinia, Arabia, and Egypt the development of the religion of Amen was taking a new color and new expression and even in China and among the Huns new religious ideas were revealed. This will give us a little idea of how the religious and the ethical, moral, artistic, and scientific development of man has progressed in cycles just as the changes in the continents have changed in cycles and that at certain definite periods of the past two hundred thousand years, there were worldwide and universal revelations in religious and philosophical thought as though the great Cosmic Mind, which the Lemurians recognized as the ruling system of the world, preordained such revelations as the evolution of man and made him ready or qualified for the coming of new knowledge and new life.

The development of the Brahman religion and philosophy led into the birth and leadership of Buddha among men of his country as an inspired messenger of God. This was around the 5th century B.C., and coincident with this Cosmic or divinely inspired incident of religious life there was born Confucius, as a leader of the Chinese, Cyrus, the leader of the Iranians and the Chaldeans, and others in other lands, including Pythagoras among the Greeks. This would indicate that inspired leaders among men were born and carried on their great missions at certain well defined cycles of time as a universal condition of human development.

After the 3rd or 4th century B.C., the Indian empire developed in strength and power until there were various invasions, changes of religion, and deaths of great leaders in the 4th and 5th centuries A.D.

This resulted in the diminishing of the Indian empire and through the invasion of the Moslems the empire continued to weaken in its great strength and beauty.

The Huns were a small race that made a bitter fight in the early centuries to maintain their distinction and power but the continuous raids by the Mongolians and outlying tribes of central Asia greatly weakened them. Finally many treaties were made by Chinese emperors and these Huns of northern China, known as the Tartars, strengthened their civilization and were able to protect themselves against the raids of so-called Barbarians; but they were finally defeated by the Chinese Emperor Mu-wang about 1000 B.C., and the inter-mixing with the Chinese undermined the imperial authority and the people as a nation almost passed out of existence and power in the 6th century B.C. Finally the Tartars or Huns made raids on China and through the contact with other people, the Huns, the Tartars, and other nomads of the Gobi desert were driven west by prolonged wars. However, about the 3rd century B.C., they advanced across the Volga and forced the Ostro-Goths and Teutonic tribes into central Europe but later united with them against the Romans and Franks. About the 4th century B.C., Attila became their great leader and strengthened their empire enormously. After his death the Hun empire settled permanently in South Russia, Hungary, and Bulgaria. They attempted further invasions in the 5th and 6th century A.D., but for hundreds of years remained relatively a weak power until we find this power developing again in Russia and the Tartars and Mongolians revealing the power of their early ancestors.

The Chinese, as the last of the eight principal classifications of the races of man in the year 2000, were perhaps the most interesting because of the many unique features of their language, customs, habits, and religion. Their empire at this time was divided into nine provinces under the autocratic rule of one emperor. This form of political government was a slight modification of the ancient Lemurian government. Their greatest development was in the form of militarism but this was soon abandoned as the most important power, and philosophy and scientific knowledge supplanted militarism. They had kept, perhaps, the most perfect records of ancient times and valued so highly their well-traced origin among the Lemurians that their religion took on the form of ancestral worship, and this was molded into doctrines by the Emperor Yao in the year 1550 B.C. It is interesting to note that the first handwritten documents of a reliable and dependable nature were possessed by the Chinese and they were already tabulated and indexed in the year 1500 B.C., when a new form of philosophy and cultural development had its birth. The power of the Chinese empire developed magnificently and became the center of 1700 small feudal states under an imperial sovereign in the year 1200 B.C. From then on their art, literature, and science increased, and their literary writings and scientific notations show that their knowledge foreshadowed many of the discoveries of modem science. They became unusually wonderful workers in bronze, and art in metal. When Confucius was born his teachings solidified all of the ancient philosophies and ancient ideals and became the standard for the customs and politics, as well as religion of the life of China for its entire future. The history of China from that period on to the present, is too well-known to require any comments in this book.

Viewing the races of man today and their empires, nations, and countries, we find that many have descended from these which I have just described. By turning to any encyclopedia and looking up the description of any race of people or any existing nation, one will find references to their origin as associated with the tribes and races described in the foregoing paragraphs.

If we should expect to find, however, any pure blooded Lemurians existing today we would have to seek for them among those who had descended from the first Lemurians and had remained on land and in climate as near like the early continent of Lemuria as possible, and had refrained from intermarriage with many modified tribes that had descended from them in other parts of the world. In other words, in seeking for the purest tribe of Lemurians we would have to seek for men and women who had married among those of their own closest branch of descendants and who had remained in similar environment and conditions of living. There is only one place in the world today where parts of the ancient continent of Lemuria have remained with little change in regard to environment of living. There is only one place in the world today where parts of the ancient continent of Lemuria have remained with little change in regard to environment and climate, and in seeking here for any remnants of the Lemurians we have been fortunate in finding those who are representatives of the purest type and who have lived for thousands of years in the same locality with a minimum amount of intermarriage and external influence. These people we shall speak of in a future chapter.

MYSTERIOUS CALIFORNIA

We can find mystery and romance in the lives of nations and countries as well as in the lives of individuals, and, perhaps, of all the strange and mysterious parts of the world there is none that is so filled with the elements of fascinating and alluring mystery as that of the country of California.

I use the word *country* very advisably because the more one becomes acquainted with the State of California, its history, its traditions, its heritage, and its people of today with their inherited customs and interesting habits of living, the more one is convinced that the personal sentiments regarding California as are public are more deeply seated than most Americans realize.

It often surprises those who go from various parts of the world, and especially those who go to this new land from eastern parts of the United States, to find that California is still very proud of the former flag of its Republic and that on every holiday and at every fiesta occasion— which means very frequently, indeed—the flag of the Republic of California is displayed alongside of the American flag.

There is no other State in the Union, perhaps, in which the school children are taught so many songs that praise the glories of California and pay tribute to its ancient and present day virtues and where such songs are sung not only by the children but by the adults in their theaters, by the members of the various service clubs, and by large conclaves wherever they may be assembled. The ancient spirit of gaiety and gala festivities is still so alive in the hearts of the Californians that the least excuse — the visit of some government official, the visit of some foreign diplomat, or commander of a foreign vessel, the flying through the fair skies of some unusual aviator, the discovery of some new field or mountain of gold, the anniversary of some old Spanish or California event—is the occasion for wonderful parades, gay holiday celebrations with the schools closed, the business institutions semi-active, and the governors, mayors, city councilors, and leading citizens taking part with elaborate, flowered floats, the wearing of Spanish costumes by most of the citizens, the selection of local queens to rule over mythical courts, community dancing on the streets in the evening and every other form of festivity for which the ancient periods of its history were famous. There is a sweet loveliness about the spirit of the people, accompanied by a broad toleration for all view-points, for all religions, all customs, and habits, and a united determination to make life worth living and to make the enjoyment of life a primary motive rather than a secondary one. This has had no detrimental effect upon business but has, in fact, stimulated it; and whereas in eastern sections of the United States the drive for money and big business is considered necessary as a primary objective in order to avoid complete disruption of business, the Californians have proved that the very reverse may be true.

The extreme contrasts in its climate, its scenery, the spirit of its people, so far as present day matters are concerned, and the thousands of variations and gradations that lie between these extremes, constitute a combination of conditions that helps to make California so attractive. While one may bask in warm sunlight on its beaches at any period of the year, one may also journey for a few hours by automobile or train to its mountain tops and in summer attire, with all the attractive clothing of the sport wear of the polo field, enjoy the thrills of snowballing and skiing. From fertile green valleys filled with thousands of varieties of wild flowers and roses, and from plains trampled by herds of thousands of head of cattle, or desert places of wind blown sand that afford the opportunity for the making of pictures with Sahara settings, one may journey in a few hours to the highest peaks surrounded by rugged scenery, or into forests that are so dense that many of them have never been explored and are natural museums of research. Every hour spent in driving or riding, walking or boating on California lands, or in the streams, lakes, bays or the Ocean, brings continuous surprises and an ever changing panorama of new interest and new thrills.

To the stranger, California is still the land of gold— the golden poppy in the fields and the many other golden flowers, along with the golden colors of peaches, apricots, apples and other fruits, the gold in the sky at sunset that lasts long into the evening, the golden reflections in the waters, the golden tints of the Spanish homes, the golden colorings in the tapestries, drapes, awnings, curtains and other decorative material, and the gold in the soil that seems to have no limit for those who persevere in seeking for it, constantly impresses the stranger with the fact that not one tenth of California has been explored nor converted into the marvelous opportunities that lie before it.

But, what interests those of a scientific or philosophical turn of mind to a greater degree than its gold or spirit of joy and happiness, health and invigoration, are the many mysteries and the stories of ancient times that one hears in every part of this unusual country. As those from the east approach California and ride over the long spaces of almost desert areas or lands of ranches and unfertile valleys to the foothills of the Sierras one feels that one is going to a far distant place that must be different and unlike any thing passed on the way. Ascending the foothills to the top of the Sierra Range one enters into the snow and cold of the higher regions in winter with its barrenness, or into the heavy vegetation and forest growth of the summer. Then begins the decline, minute after minute, in the interesting, twisting, turning, railroad ride down the sides of the Sierra Nevada Mountains to the glories of California. On every hand one sees the remnants and relies of the days of '49 when the miners hastily erected cabins and buildings, while others worked in bringing forth the fortune that proved the ancient stories of California to be true. The snow gradually disappears, the valleys become more fertile, the flowers appear with fields even though the rest of the country that has been left behind is covered with frost. As each minute brings the traveler further west into California and toward the Pacific Coast, he notices that the soil is rapidly changing, the trees are different, the rock formations are distinctive and picturesque, thousands of wild flowers of varieties never seen in the east become more profuse. Blossoms, ferns, palms and plants that grow only in the hot houses of the east or can be raised only under careful culture are seen growing wildly without any cultivation or special attention. The climate becomes mild, the spirit of the people seems to be one of joy. There is an invigoration in the air which gradually impresses the stranger with a feeling that there are vibrations of some mysterious vitality, of something very old, very antique, romantic and unfathomable.

The stranger, therefore, is never surprised when the first citizen of this western Republic begins to tell him of the uncommon things to be seen or even heard in the day time or the night.

I am aware of the fact that no Chamber of Commerce in any of the very progressive cities of California would think of writing a book about the local allurements of each community by giving any emphasis to the weird sights, strange sounds or peculiar mysteries within its own boundaries. To the public at large these things may have no appeal, and to some they might be objection able. But to the lover of mystery, the student of the sciences, the research worker, the thinker, and those intellectually inclined, the mysteries of California are not only appealing but never completely solved and never forgotten.

One just passes from one interesting situation, one astonishing condition, one fascinating story or experience, to another, day after day and mile after mile as one rides or walks along the King"s Highway of California, called "El Camino Real." And, even where this old trail ends the Indian paths going northward or eastward leading one into even deeper fantasies of interest that equal those found in the fairy tales of our childhood.

Are all of these stories merely traditions handed down from early generations and having no foundation in fact? Are the tales and reports of strange occurrences only the imaginations of a people still moved by the emotions of their ancestors? Are all these things purely fictional and part of the fiesta spirit? A stay of but a month in this wonderful state convinces anyone that all of the stories and experiences are probably true, and that most of them are told with little elaboration and little fiction. The spell of the California mysteries gradually overpowers the visitor who prolongs his stay, and therein lies the secret of the universal enthusiasm for its land that every native son and daughter expresses so convincingly.

Those who have read the preceding chapters of this book will realize that the State of California actually represents the oldest habitated, cultivated, civilized land on the face of the earth that is still in practically the same physical form, and in the same environment, as when God first created it. I have already said that science recognizes the fact that in the forests of California, in the hills and valley s, in the rock and shell of its great mountains, and in the sand and soil of its shores are found the oldest living things in the world; and so far as specimens of non-living matter, relies of bye-gone, forgotten, prehistoric times are concerned, California offers the greatest abundance of evidence, and with such fascinating pictures as quicken the emotion of romance, the spirit of imagination, and the heartbeat of weird thrills.

For instance, one may journey to that beautiful little city known as Santa Barbara, where only a few years ago a mild earthquake completed some of the final adjustments of the land upon which it is situated, and which adjustment began at the time that the continent of Lemuria was submerged. Here in a beautiful spot with magnificent homes built along the shore drive, reminding one of the Riviera of France and Italy, and with a busy city constantly in fiesta dress, we have the setting of a very ancient habitation, the mystery of which is yet unsolved. O ff the shore of this unique city, modem in its progressive architecture and American beauty and antique in the many Spanish homes and ancient structures, there are several islands whose stories no man can tell in detail but which may some day bring millions of visitors to their shores that they may say that they have seen such memorable places in the western world. For these islands were at one time the fortified preserves of an ancient race whose homes and daily activities occupied the district of the mainland where the city of Santa Barbara now rests. Because, however, of the continued invasions by unknown tribes from South America, unknown people from the north, and, stranger still, the people from far inland, they lived exclusively by themselves with a language, a complexion, a code of living, and an architecture distinctly their own, unlike anything else in the rest of the world.

All that they held dear and all that they could save and gather of worldly value to protect them in the future days of inevitable conquest they stored on the islands and fortified these to a degree that astonishes the creators of our modem forms of fortification. These people, known technically as a tribe with the name Chumash, constituted practically an independent race of people, so far as their ancestry would appear in ordinary records of anthropology, but, as the reader will divine, they were one of a number of groups or tribes of separated communities that were direct descendants of the Lemurians, continuing to live in their own land without intermarrying with other tribes or allowing the blood that flowed in their veins to be blended with any other.

Thus, it was inevitable that the race should disappear, just as the other groups of similar descendants in other parts of California are gradually disappearing. When Cabrillo discovered these Chumash natives in 1542 there were over 35,000 of them, and in 1771 when missionary work entered into their lives and a tabulation was accurately made there were 8,960 remaining, and in 1900 three families constituting nine adults remained, while today but one of these adults is living, and he has been taken by his Lemurian brethren into another community. Science admits that these people were well-versed and well-developed in the art of sea life, and technically expert in harpooning and spear-throwing. Others in their community revealed, even in 1542, a long culture and experience in art, pottery making, architecture, basket weaving, astronomy, the sciences generally, and especially what they called the art of healing and the prevention and cure of diseases. If ever the proper expeditionary work and research efforts are made in the soil of the islands off the coast of Santa

Barbara and in the deep soil underlying the present city there will be rich rewards made to the history of man and the history of this great State; but this is only one of the many spots in California that offers the novelist, the scientist, the dreamer, and the artist a golden opportunity.

Of the largest of the groups of descendants of Lemurians, still living and constituting one of the most impenetrable mysteries of the State, I will speak in another chapter; but there are other interesting places in California which one can touch upon only lightly for the complete details of each would fill many volumes.

In the first place, California is really much like an island continent of itself, that is, if we add Oregon and Washington to the State of California and likewise the peninsula known as Lower California, for in ancient times all of this was known as California. The soil, the climate, the products of the soil, and everything in and around the land of these several States are so different and so distinctly unique in comparison with the rest of the United States that we may look upon this group of States as constituting a separate nation or a separate island. We are warranted in this view-point by the fact that this territory was at one time an island separate and distinct from the rest of the North American continent.

The name California itself gives us the first due to the mystery and romance of the West. For years there were many and varied explanations as to where the name California came from, and how it came to be applied to this western land. We know that most, if not all, of the other names used in the State and which are foreign to the American language, were copied from European languages, mostly Spanish, and the Padres and the missionaries. But the name California has no definite meaning in any European language and is quite a unique name in itself.

It was Rev. Edward Everett Haie who discovered in 1862 a due to the origin of the name California and how it came to be applied to this western land. He found in his researches that just before California became the goal of foreign expeditions, especially those of a Spanish nature, there was reprinted in Spain a story of chivalry that had once been very popular in the time of the Crusades but which had come down from great antiquity as a story of traditional exploits and scientific research. This story in its new and revised form became extremely popular and in it there was described, with all of the grandeur and romance of the pre-Crusade days, a land in the western waters in the form of a great island ruled by the beautiful heroine of the story known as *Queen Califa*, and the island over which she ruled was called *California*.

The description in the story stated that this wonderful island was on "the right hand of the Indies, very near to the terrestrial paradise." The description of the people was quite mythical and romantic but there was every evidence in the story that it was based upon expeditions made by those who, in prehistoric times, had been able to reach the shores of this island and studied its people and explored the nature of its country and soil. The reference to it as being near the *terrestrial paradise* is typical of other ancient records which referred to the existing remnants of Lemuria as the early paradise of man, the Garden of Eden, and the birthplace and cradle of all races of man. The references to the vast amount of gold that could be found in this island of *California*, the quiet, peaceful waters which surrounded it, its abundance of fruit and rich vegetation, its wonderful climate, and the cordiality of its people, ever made the story an unforgettable one and was unquestionably responsible for the many hundreds of expeditions from various parts of the eastern and western world which made this island their goal.

In this regard the reader should bear in mind that the expedition of Columbus was very late, indeed, and that long before Vespucci made his discoveries and long before any expeditions were made of which we have any popular record or any definite information at all, there were thousands of expeditions to this western world when North and South America as continents were not in the position now occupied by them, and when the so-called island of California was all that was left of the eastern edge of the submerged continent of Lemuria. As an instance of how the idea persisted through many centuries in the consciousness of man regarding the country of *California* being an island separate from any continent at all, I offer in evidence, a drawing made from the famous *Nancy Globe*. This globe was seen in the town library at Nancy, France, where it has been for many years, and its recorded history dates back to 1531, although the actual date of its making is not known. It is but six inches in diameter and was highly colored, and considered very accurate and complete for the period in which it was made. Such maps or globes as these were made not by navigators themselves but by those deep students of research who specialized in watching and recording the explorations of navigators and of special expeditions. They tried to put into one map the facts and figures, the findings and the dates brought back to the old world by the scores of capable observers and explorers. In studying this map one will quickly notice that although the continent of North and South America is fairly accurately drawn and represents North America as being the larger Spanish land with the country of New Spain in the Southern part, and eastern Asia and India in the western part, there is no attempt to make the peninsula of California a part of the mainland but rather to show all of California or the western part of the continent of North America as a separate island with a group of small islands at its Southern extremity. In other words, nothing that had been reported by the early explorers at the time that this globe was made changed the opinion and belief of all the explorers and map makers that California was a land separate from North America.

The Nancy Globe

In order to understand why California was considered an island, your attention is called to Map No. 4. This is a sketch of the land that unquestionably constituted the island remnant of the eastern end of the continent of Lemuria after it submerged and as it was being united to the western coast of the North American continent. By examining this map one will find that this island section was composed of a small mountain range along the western shore line and of a larger mountain range, comprising the Cascade and Sierra Nevada Mountains, on the eastern shore of the island, and that these mountains united and again divided near the Southern part forming the peninsula of Lower California and part of the Mexican coast line. In the north the island ended in swamplands, while the island of Vancouver was a swampy marsh in a bay.

Lying between the two mountain ranges of this island of California was a low valley most of which was occupied by a bay, with its center opposite what is now the Bay of San Francisco, near the Golden Gate. This means that the Santa Clara, San Joaquin, and Sacramento Valleys were at one time under water and that even preceding this period the northern part of the island of California, up to and a little way beyond the northern boundary line of the present State of California, was under water forming a very large inland bay. These waters remained for perhaps fifteen or twenty thousand years, but gradually receded through the continued rising of the island of California, and through volcanic and earthquake effects upon the general surface of the land. The present Bay of San Francisco, and much of the swamplands in the Sacramento Valley, are remnants of this ancient bay, while the beautiful and fertile Valley of Santa Clara is a result of the many centuries of watery deposits and earthly compositions resulting from the existence of the great bay and its gradual change, so that, today, the Santa Clara Valley with its sea shells deeply embedded in its soil and the eternal marks of the effects of water upon the hill sides around the valley, gives mute evidence of what once existed; and the marvelous products of fruit and flowers found in this valley and constituting a wealth that is equal to the gold found in the mountains shows how nature can prepare and arrange its blessing for man.

Situated in the center of this wonderful valley is that fascinating city of *San Jose*, where the first pueblo was established after the Padres, and the early explorers preceding them, had selected this site as the most beautiful and most suitable for the building of a great city in the center of perfect climate. This city, then, became the first Capitol of the State and the first center of the great Spanish life and wealthiest estates ever known in California. A visit to San Jose today, and a ride through its brilliantly illuminated, busy, modem, business streets reminds one of a ride through the busy section of the largest eastern cities, for the same spirit of progressiveness, the same leadership in advance of other communities is found, and the representation of many great eastern industries gives a very distinct atmosphere to the business and social life of this old city. Yet, in the heart of it, and its environs, lie many fascinating, alluring and fantastic stories and earmarks of ancient times.

Here we find the very center of the California fiestas, the flowery parades, the celebrations, the gaiety and happy social life of the old and the new world combined. Still, in its progressiveness it has attracted to it more universities and colleges and institutions of learning than any other city of its size in the West, and many of these date to great antiquity. Even the famous *Leland Stanford University*, now located further north in Palo Alto, had its early foundation in San Jose. And, just up on the mountains which adjoin San Jose is located the great Lick Observatory, while on the northern boundaries of the city, in the famous *Santa Clara University* is that other well-known observatory where the Padre of the Rains has made his calculations and his discoveries of world-wide interest.

Not far from San Jose and just across a little mountain range called the *Santa Cruz Mountains* is a small peninsula which stands unique in romantic, religious history, for here is the mountain of Carmel, the valley of Carmel, and the Carmel River. The Carmelites who came here and established a monastery were acquainted with this particular locality long before Viscaino made his expeditions and brought scientists, Padres, and some *Rosicrucian mystics* to this region to unite their efforts in further amplifying the modifications and civilization of the Carmel and Santa Clara valleys. The early expeditions to California had reported that there was a bay and a small peninsula along the western coast that resembled the Bay of Acre with its peninsula, its Mount of Carmel and the Carmel River running inland; and the further facts were that these two similar bays and peninsulas were in almost the same latitude, with similar climates and similar vegetation, although in almost opposite parts of the world. It was for this reason that the mystic descendants of an early mystery school located in Carmel of the East desired to accompany the expedition to the New World, and named the goal of their expedition Carmel long before they reached its shores. The early records of these mystics, known as *Rosicrucians*, show that the establishment of the Carmelites as a religious order followed the selection of this site for the establishment of the first Rosicrucian Temple on the Pacific shores, equaling a similar foundation laid by the Rosicrucian pilgrims on the eastern shore in what is now known as the city of Philadelphia in 1694.

It is an interesting fact that many of the trees and shrubs found growing in profusion in the valley and mountains of this new western-world Carmel were unknown in any other part of the world several centuries ago, except near the river of Carmel on the Bay of Acre. The valley of Carmel in California and its entire environment is filled with romantic stories and stories of mystery and Cosmic weirdness. It is not surprising, therefore, that the valley contains a little town known as Carmel-by-the-Sea, which holds itself separate from the mad progress of western civilization and shelters cozy little cottages and studios where the best known writers and artists of the world have come and, like Robert Louis Stevenson, have stayed for months or years and written their greatest novels or painted their greatest pictures; for here in this strange village nestled among the pines, and sitting in a veritable garden of flowers, one is easily inspired by the very vibrations of the place, as well as by the stories and historical records which are available in its little cabin library.

Not far from San Jose, close to the sea shore, near the attractive mountains, and practically on the main highway of the State, Carmel with the beaches of Monterey and Del Monte, constitute a combination of attractions where the investigators of historic traditions and archaeological research find the greatest joy of life.

Even in the centuries of long ago when much of this State was wild and uncivilized, so to speak, the ancient people of Lemuria, finding their great continent submerging beneath the water and their people being wiped out of earthly existence by the greatest of all floods and catastrophes, scattered into the valleys and mountainsides of this eastern portion of their continent which seemed to be rising higher. Here they laid foundations, built structures, created conditions, and established perpetual memorials to their highly advanced civilization.

Much of the mute testimony to their knowledge and wisdom is beyond our comprehension even today and many of their accomplishments remain unexplained by science and unduplicated by all of our progressiveness. Month after month visitors and explorers in California come face to face with some great rock of strange carving, some magnificent piece of sculptured work lying beneath age-old shrubbery or some skeleton or the remains of some living creature which awes them and leaves them spell-bound in the realization of our ability to understand.

Whoever the Queen Califa may have been that ruled over a land so full of gold that the poorest and most common of her subjects were found literally covered with gold ornamentations, she must have ruled over a highly illuminated and happy nation of people, and if in analyzing her descendants who still live in California we find any due to that which made this civilization so old and so great, we may find the key to that which still makes California the land of gold.

PRESENT DAY MYSTIC LEMURIANS IN CALIFORNIA

*I*t has been stated in preceding chapters, the great catastrophes that overwhelmed the continent of Lemuria and caused the final submergence of nearly all of it in more or less rapid time, forced the surviving remnants of the great race of civilized inhabitants to flee to the highest mountain tops and seek there a possible haven.

Whether many went to upper plateaus of high mountains and were eventually thrown into the sea and lost to earthly life, we do not know, except that millions of beings lost their lives in the great catastrophes, but probably most of these were living in the peaceful valleys and plains of the great continent.

The evidence shows that the eastern portion of the continent of Lemuria, or that portion nearest to the North American continent, was very high and naturally appeared to be the best place for those who were given time and opportunity to reach these points and establish themselves in safety. The fact that only a few thousand succeeded in reaching the mountains would indicate that the last great catastrophe of Lemuria was more or less sudden and decidedly complete in its submergence of the land. Even those high eastern mountains that remained above water were greatly lowered in height, for before the catastrophe they were probably as high as any to be found in the world. The nature of the soil around these mountains indicates that for many centuries the lowest valleys on either side of the mountains were high above sea level, and then for many centuries were lowered beneath sea level and completely submerged. A later series of minor earth changes raised the valleys sufficiently high enough to drain them of the water and leave them in the condition in which we find the valley of Santa Clara for instance, at the present time.

Because of the rapidity of the submergence and the evident extent of the catastrophe those few thousand who were able to reach the hillsides and attain a height of safety were unable to bring with the many great quantity of their personal effects and very little of their stores of supplies. However, the records indicate that anticipating this possibility they had arranged and prepared for the eventual catastrophe by establishing small, conservative, and well-protected bases of supplies in various sections of the high mountains. These protected places were constructed in the typical Lemurian style out of very hard stone and marble, and being built for permanency and to survive the most severe storms and conditions of climate, they are today in their partly ruined condition, the only surviving examples of Lemurian architecture of the pure type.

This accounts for the occasional discovery of strangely built structures found in a ruined condition by explorers in the mountains of California. Often the ruins are of small buildings and so torn asunder by storms and the handiwork of later tribes who used much of the stone for the building of new structures that little of the original design or plan remains. But, in other parts of California and especially in the vast forests and unexplored regions, many moss-covered, shrubbery-hidden ruins have been accidentally found by explorers who have made their first reports in great astonishment, but were later prevented by mysterious forces and strange incidents from returning to these sites and making any further investigations.

I remember speaking to one such explorer who was not given to any degree of romance or emotionalism in his profound scientific work, who said that the frequent frustrations of his scientific investigations by weird and almost uncanny incidents made him think, in one of his moments of reverie, that there was a sleeping personality in the highest regions of the Sierras like the traditional personality of Rip Van Winkle sleeping in the Catskill Mountains, and that whenever an investigator approached this sleeping personality too closely it awakened and thundered forth its protests. While he was speaking allegorically it reminded me of the fact that it was almost a literal explanation of what had actually occurred in many parts of the State.

There are mountainous parts of California where men go lion hunting or hunting for other wild animals, and where the foot of a white man has probably never trod for many centuries, if at all. It is not uncommon for these hunters, and for lonely explorers in search of thrills and excitement, to come face to face with peculiar conditions, unexpected scenes, and gruesome relies of ancient peoples. Many very valuable specimens of human forms and of animals of all species have been found in remote parts of these mountains and are preserved today in many museums of the country.

More thrilling than these stories of scientific discoveries are the stories of personal experiences on the part of tourists who love to enter into the wild parts of any country seeking the personal pleasure of discovering new things. Their stories when told at the fire-sides of the bungalows or in the clubs of the social classes in the larger cities, sound like tales from foreign lands of ancient times. The accumulation of these stories with a careful analysis and comparison of them shows such similarity of details and such consistency in principles as to convince one that they are founded upon truth. It is interesting, therefore, to spend time in visiting some of the unusual places of the mountains of California and studying the relies of ancient civilization. Even when we go north of California into other states we find similar conditions, proving that all of these western states which constituted the island of California at one time, were occupied by identical people with identical customs and habits.

One of the interesting explorations to be made with safety and pleasure by any visitor to California is in the Basin of Klamath Falls. The great Klamath Basin is in Oregon but this is only a remnant of the great inland sea that one time reached far down into the present State of California, and the present Klamath Lake reaches across the

Oregon State line into the northern part of California and occupies only a small portion of the land in the north eastern corner of Siskiyou County, whereas at one time this lake reached down through this county into the adjoining one. Into this lake there projects at the present time a small peninsula which is the remnant of a high mountain where was located one of the colonies of the surviving Lemurians. On the rocks of this peninsula are carved the strangest marks that modem scientists have ever attempted to interpret. There are thousands of these hieroglyphic characters and I have drawn a few of the principal figures and reproduce them here as samples of the Klamath Falls' writing.

KLAMATH FALLS WRITING

Those who have attempted to interpret the hundreds of feet of these characters on the stones in various sections surrounding the lake have discovered that there is a uniformity to the writing. They have not been able to evolve an alphabet or a code which will reveal the messages written there which were intended to inform future generations regarding the nature of the colony surrounding this lake and the story of their catastrophe and struggles for life. I have found in these characters, however, a similarity to many of the other Lemurian characters to which reference has been made and the important key throughout these writings is the various forms in which the cross appears. Of this I will speak later. It is interesting to note that from ancient times certain parts of this country surrounding the lake and the Klamath Falls Basin have had peculiar names. A century ago these names were believed to be names which the Indian tribes gave to the places and they were considered to be Indian names, but a careful study of them shows that they were in use long before the Indians could have settled in any part of this country and are not

Indian names at all. Scientists have decided that the 1,200 feet or more of carved writings are on rocks that have been below and above water at different periods and that, therefore, the writings were made many hundreds of years ago. Different generations have added to these writings in order to bring the history of their people up to a very modem date, comparatively speaking. One of the other interesting facts is that the Sacred Oak of the ancient Druid mystic brotherhood appears in these writings, in many significant places; and in other places the Sacred Lamp of the Druids appears. The Druids eventually had their center of earthly activities in the British lands about the beginning of the Christian era. In addition to this evidence of relation with the Druids, there is very positive evidence that the writers of these strange characters where those who helped to establish the Sanskrit language and the Roman language and were, therefore, part of the highly cultured and civilized races that spread the most modem of literary culture in various parts of the world.

For instance, part of the lake valley was known to the Modoc Indians who lived there in later generations as "The Valley of Knowledge" because there was every evidence that this place had been the seat of learning for some ancient tribes of people. These American Indians called this valley of knowledge the "Walla-Was-Skeeny." The Indians said that this meant, "Valley of Knowledge" but it was found that these words were not like any other words in their Indian language or dialect,

Then it was discovered that these Indians had inherited this name, or had received it from the descendants of the early tribes who were still living there when the Indians came and that the words, "Walla-Was-Skeeny" was really an attempt to pronounce the Latin words meaning *valley of knowledge* or *Vallis Scientia*. It was also found that these Modoc Indians had inherited the word "wocus" for the name of the lily, while in Latin it is lotus. The ruins of a former walled-in preserve built by the Lemurians on the top of a mountain north of Olene in Klamath County was called "moynia" by the Modoc Indians, and in Latin any walled-in place, or the site of ramparts, is called *moynia*. Some of the hills in this region are called "collil" and the Latin word for hills of this nature is collis. On the other hand, some Greek words appear in the language also for there is another mountain point which the Indians claim was called "Mu-Pi." These two syllables are easily recognized as two letters of the Greek alphabet.

It may be said in passing that when the American Indians were first discovered in this part of California and the writing observed by early explorers, the Indians disclaimed any knowledge regarding the origin of the writing or any interpretation of even a part of it, and students of the various Indian dialects and forms of writing say that this ancient writing is totally unlike anything that any of the American Indian tribes produced.

It has been reported that many years ago the region near these strange writings was illuminated at night with peculiar white lights, and all investigation failed to reveal any origin or source for such illumination. At that time electricity was not available in that district and there were no indications of fires of any kind being built on the soil or on any of the rocks.

This element of strange lights enters very freely in the mysteries of California. In many parts of the State on certain nights of each month mountain peaks are illuminated, or in between the trees of great forests a strange white light almost like the white light of a photographer's flashlight is seen, not in sudden flashes or explosions but in a steady manner lasting for several hours. Every manner of research has failed to trace the real source of these lights. For instance, within the past year a very old white light seen forty or fifty years ago, and considered as gone forever during the past twenty years or more, has suddenly reappeared in the foothills east of San Jose within a mile or two of the San Jose Mission. This great white light, many hundreds of feet below the valley of Santa Clara, appears to be in the midst of a dense forest and rising above the trees. It is clearly seen from various parts of the San Francisco Bay.

At first this great white light was believed by many to be a signal of some kind produced by illegal makers of alcoholic liquors, probably for the purpose of signaling to some small craft in the bay. Investigation made during the day failed to reveal any structure, home, house, or cave anywhere near the area where the light was seen, nor any indication of a fire of any kind. Finally surveyors were engaged and transits were set pointing to the exact location of the white light as seen at night and in the day time these transits pointed very definitely to a dense group of trees on the mountain side barren of all homes, with no indication of even burnt leaves on the ground. Electricity is not available in this district of the mountains and how such a steady light could be produced for a long time without leaving any trace of itself is one of the unsolved mysteries still occupying the attention of hundreds of keen intellects. On the other hand, as proof that these lights may be associated with some of the mysteries of Lemuria and its people, the weird stories of Mt. Shasta in California remain as an ever-lasting fascination.

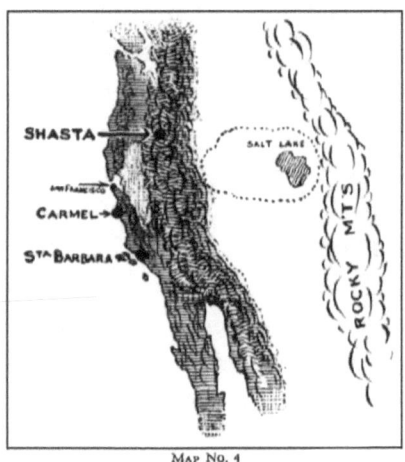

Map No. 4

Mt. Shasta is located at the northern extremity of the Sierra Nevada Mountain Range. It is, therefore, located in Siskiyou County, not many miles from the Klamath Lake area to which I have just referred. Mt. Shasta is the cone of an extinct volcano rising to a height of over 14,000 feet above sea level. Scientists point out the mute evidence of archaeology, showing that its deep-fluted sides prove that at one time it was much higher than it is now and that the ground around it has sunken, and the mountain itself has been worn away in glacial periods by the action of ice. There are other mountains nearby which are only a little over 9,000 feet above sea level and which bear evidence that today they are mere remnants of their former greatness. Mt. Shasta is still possible of eruption because a true sulfurous furole lies just below the extreme summit and one or two others on its northern slope emit heat, smoke, and other elements, proving that some day there may be one more final, though very mild, eruption from one part of this volcano.

At one time, however, Mt. Shasta was undoubtedly the highest of all the mountain peaks in this part of California. It is a beautiful sight, with its upper regions covered with snow most of the year, and can be seen from many great distances. The streams of water in and around this area are of an unusual quality and the soil is exceedingly productive when irrigated, being of very ancient origin like the remaining parts of California. To the east of this volcano is the well-known Shasta Forest. The heart of the forest is less than thirty miles from the foot of the volcano, and in the area lying between the two is low land, believed to be traversed by a number of fine streams and brooks. Little is known of this region lying between Shasta and the forest, but it is most certainly a marked spot in the minds of thousands of persons who have witnessed the strange sights to be seen from nearby points of vantage.

For several hundred years or more the old timers living in northern California, and many tourists, explorers, government officials, scientists, novelists, artists, writers, and those merely inquisitive, have centered their attention upon the strange happenings in this region. Many years ago it was quite common to hear stories whispered in northern California about the occasional, strange looking, persons seen to emanate from the forests and the dense growth of trees in that region and who would run back into hiding when discovered or seen by anyone. Occasionally one of these oddly dressed individuals would come to one of the smaller towns and trade nuggets and gold dust for some modem commodities. These odd looking persons were not only peculiar in their dress and different in attire from any costume ever seen on the American Indian, and especially the California Indian, but distinctive in features and complexion; tall, graceful and agile, having the appearance of being quite old and yet exceedingly virile. They gave every indication of being what one would term a foreigner, but with a larger head, much larger forehead, a headdress that had a special decoration that came down over the center of the forehead to the bridge of the nose, and thus hid or covered a part of the forehead that many have attempted to see and study. At other times great fires were seen to be burning in the center of the woods, allowing the blue and white illumination to penetrate the darkness between the trees; between the fire and the observer strange figures were seen to pass at times, silhouetted against the great light.

At other times when the wind was blowing in the proper direction strange chanting and singing, and weird, beautiful music would float or be carried in the direction of one of the smaller cities or towns nearby.

Every attempt by investigators to invade this district and observe what was going on resulted in a similar experience, and the similarity of these experiences related by persons who had never come in contact with those who might have informed them, is one of the outstanding pieces of evidence regarding the truthfulness of the whole story. Invariably the investigator was considered an intruder, and after having reached a certain point in his progress toward the center of the lights and sounds, he would either come in contact with a very heavily covered and concealed person of large size who would lift him up and push him away from the district, as though being forcibly impressed with the idea to hurry away as rapidly as possible, or a strange and peculiar set of vibrations or invisible energy, would seem to emanate toward the investigator and force him to remain fixed in his position and to be able to move in no other direction than away from the place of his inquiry. Thus the conditions and the mysterious facts were whispered and talked about for many years until that well-known scientist, Professor Edgar Lucin Larkin, Director of *Mt. Lowe Observatory* in Southern California, accidentally discovered a few new facts about this northern California mystery.

While he was engaged in experimenting with a new feature of one of the long distance telescopes used for auxiliary purposes in his observatory, he turned it north and south of his location along the top of the mountain range on which the observatory was established many years ago, merely for the purpose, as he said, of testing its daytime usefulness and to help him in gauging a new standard scale for determining distances. He claims that he had never heard of the mystery about Shasta and probably would have taken little interest in it if he had heard of it. He picked out Mt. Shasta, however, as an object upon which to focus his vision, because through this telescope the high snowcapped top of Shasta stood out clearly against the deep blue sky. After he had consulted the maps of California and determined in miles and feet the exact distance between himself and the peak of Shasta and made his notations for the purpose of comparing these figures with the new scale of relative distances upon which he was working, he moved the telescope so that its field of vision included the lower eastern side of Shasta and, anticipating that he would see only the tops of trees in the foreground, he was surprised to see a glimmering curved surface that was truly unusual in any picture anticipated by him. As the sun shone upon this glittering object among the trees he was impressed with the thought that he was looking at a gold-tinted dome of some Oriental building. At various intervals, twenty minutes apart, he made further notations and as the sun moved in its course he gradually discovered that there were two domes rising above the tree tops near Shasta and that the part of a third one could be seen several hundred feet distant. Moving the telescope once again he found visible between the trees a corner of another structure seemingly made of marble. Knowing that there were no such structures in northern California, and especially in the land around Shasta, he left his telescope fixed to see what these things would look like in the setting sun and in darkness. He was surprised to find later in the night that around this dome were great lights, apparently white, which partially illuminated and made them visible even though there was no moon to cast any light at the time.

In his usual precise way he made careful notations regarding each peculiar thing that impressed his mind and waited for sunrise to make further observations. Another adjustment of the telescope permitted him to see smoke rising between the trees and likewise to see part of another structure. After one week's study of the matter he decided to investigate further, and it was his investigation, personally conducted, that led many scientists to explore the region to such a degree as was found possible. Others began to accumulate the facts known to those who lived nearby and it was found that at one time a very old character had emerged from this district and made some sort of important journey by foot to the city of San Francisco, where he was met by some committee of wealthy men at the Ferry Building and escorted up Market Street to the City Hall, and there some special ceremony was held to which all strangers were forbidden. Comments of those who saw the character being escorted say that never in all their lives had they seen a being of such nobility, humility, and majestic bearing in one expression. W ho he was, and what he came to do, has never been revealed and even the date of the incident is denied to all investigators; nevertheless the story is universally told and is consistent with many stories told of similar expeditions on the part of strange individuals from this district.

Many representatives of the community that must live at the foot of Mt. Shasta have been seen on the highways unexpectedly, garbed in pure white and in sandals, with long curly hair, tall and majestic in appearance, but wholly undesirous of public attention. Every attempt to photograph them and get near enough to talk to them has resulted in their sudden disappearance, either, as some have said, by their running into the shadows of forests along the highways, or as others have said, by just disappearing in the twilight.

Those who have come to stores in nearby cities, especially at Weed, have spoken English in a perfect manner with perhaps a tinge of the British accent, and have been reluctant to answer any questions or give any information about themselves. The goods they have purchased have always been paid for in gold nuggets of far greater value than the article purchased, and they have refused to accept any change indicating that to them the gold was of no value and that they had no need for money of any kind. Those who have seen some of them at their midnight ceremony around the fire claim that they have seen the silhouettes of some four or five hundred figures and that this number represents only a fraction of those grouped on one side of the fire. The origin of the fire or its nature is not known, for it does not appear to be the burning of wood or brush or of even oil or gasoline, for it is a very white light almost bordering upon a violet blueness in its brilliancy. At one part of the midnight ceremony beams of bright lights are cast upward into the trees often blazing the sky and occasionally tinging the edge of a cloud that may be hanging low. These beams of light strike against the upper portion of buildings and particularly on the domes that seem to be plated with gold. Where the buildings are illuminated and can be observed at all they appear to be constructed of marble and onyx. At sunrise another similar ceremony is conducted, attracting a great deal of attention because of the lights that appear in the darkest parts of the forest. The only key to these ceremonies that has ever been found is that which was carved upon a stone and set up near the outskirts of the forest like stelai were erected in Egypt. On one of these there were considerable hieroglyphs and underneath were cut in a careful manner the English words "Ceremony of Adoration to Guatama." The hieroglyphs indicated that the ceremony referred to was performed at sunrise, sunset, and midnight, and that the word "Guatama" meant the continent of America. An adoration ceremony of this kind would be taken to mean a celebration of appreciation, and this, therefore, must be in honor of the time when their forbears were saved from the great catastrophe by coming to this part of the mountainous region of Lemuria as it was submerging.

The stories of mystical powers attributed to these people must be taken with the proverbial grain of salt, although my reader may interpret them as he wishes. It is said, for instance, that on a number of occasions when great forest fires have raged in various parts of California and have approached close to the forest near Mt. Shasta, a strange fog has suddenly emanated from the section occupied by these peculiar people and that this fog has risen from the ground in a circular manner so as to form a circular wall around the entire area, through which the forest fires have never penetrated. Some natives in this region delight in taking the skeptic on a circular tour, pointing out to them the mute evidence shown by the burnt trees reaching a definite line that forms a circle around the mysterious region. On the inside of this circle the trees rise to great heights, of old age, and without a single scar or blemish from the burning of the trees that were destroyed within two hundred feet of them.

Others speak of having attempted to approach the region by automobile and finding that at an unexpected point where a light flashed before them their automobile refused to function properly, for the electric circuit seemed to lose its power and not until the passengers emerged from the car and backed it on the road for a hundred feet and tuned it in the opposite direction, would the electric power give any manifestation and the engine function properly. Others have said that some strange cattle, unlike anything ever seen in America, have emerged from the woods, but before going very far along the highways or by-ways these animals would be frightened by some invisible signal, and would turn abruptly around and run back toward the places from which they came.

There are hundreds of others who have testified to having seen peculiarly shaped boats which have flown out of this region high in the air over the hills and valleys of California and have been seen by others to come on to the waters of the Pacific Ocean at the shore and then to continue out on the seas as a vessel. Similar boats have been seen by seamen on the high seas, and others have seen these boats rise again in the air and go upon the land of some of the islands of the Pacific. Others have seen these peculiar vessels as far north as the Aleutian Islands. Only recently a group of persons playing golf on one of the golf lawns of California near the foothills of the Sierra Nevada Range saw a peculiar, silver-like, vessel rise in the air and float over the mountain tops and disappear. It was unlike any airship that has ever been seen and there was absolutely no noise emanating from it to indicate that it was moved by a motor of any kind.

Perhaps the most interesting explanation of what is to be found in this locality is that it is not only the ancient seat of hundreds of Lemurians who still live there and manufacture and grow all of their principal necessities and keep themselves isolated, as did the other group of Lemurians who lived at Santa Barbara many years ago, but that their village itself is only partly on the outside of Mt. Shasta, that there is a tunnel through its eastern base leading to a great enclosure in which there is a city of strange homes, and that the heat and smoke seen arising from the crater of Mt. Shasta is smoke and heat from the interior village. This is not an unusual tale, inasmuch as there are records showing that in Mexico another group of descendants from Lemuria were found living in the center of an extinct volcano, hidden from all possible worldly observation.

Thus we have one of the present day groups of Lemurians hidden in isolation in modem California, if we are to believe the testimony of reliable citizens and many scientists. It is not a story that is beyond human reason or possibility. And it is not the only strange sight or peculiar incident in California, but typical of what this old land may contain if ever it is completely and thoroughly explored.

Whether these descendants of Lemuria, as they are considered, continue to practice their ancient rites and live as they always did, or whether they have adopted some modem methods, is another question that is unanswerable. That they will eventually pass away and become extinct as the last, or one of the last, surviving groups of Lemurians, is inevitable, inasmuch as they do not allow any of their members to marry with other races.

At any rate, if all of the stories and the mute evidence of carved statuary and ruined buildings, be true, America has the honor and prestige of having on its soil the last survivors in a direct line of the first race of man on the face of the earth. Here was the beginning of that race, and here will be the end of that race. This makes America, in fact, the oldest country of the world and yet the newest, and perhaps it is this happy combination, this rare association of the old and new, this unique blending of the spirit of ancient culture with modem progressiveness, that makes the North American continent and its peoples from Canada to the Isthmus a great world of opportunity and golden fortunes.

APPENDIX I

The Cycles of Changes in the Earth

The following extracts are from a personal manuscript by John H. Tice, Meteorologist, and published privately by the officers and directors of The Meteorological Research and Publication Company of St. Louis, Missouri, in 1875.

"For half a century scientists have earnestly been laboring to discover such a cycle, but without success; yet every day the necessity for it becomes more evident and the demand for it more earnest and pressing. Professor Lockyer, an English astronomer and renowned as a spectroscopist, expresses himself upon this subject as follows: 'In Meteorology as in Astronomy, the thing is to hunt down a cycle; and if it is not to be found in the Temperate Zones, then go to the Frigid Zones, or to the Torrid Zones to look for it. If found, then above all things, and in whatever manner, lay hold of it, study it, record it, and see what it means...'

"Observation on special phenomena, such as sunspots, solar physics generally, magnetic intensity in the Earth, electric tension both o f the Earth and of the Atmosphere, auroras, earthquakes, cyclones, rainfalls and terrestrial temperatures, have been made for half a century, and some for nearly two centuries. Why these observations have not been more fruitful in valuable results is owing to the fact that each observer worked independently, and made the observations of his chosen phenomena a specialty, without ever dreaming that there was a correlation between all physical phenomena. After devoting a period to their work—equal to half the length of what the Psalmist assigns as the term of human life,— each observer came to the conclusion that his special phenomenon had a periodicity, and repeated itself in a cycle between ten and twelve years...

"After having satisfied myself of the existence of meteorological cycles, about eight years ago, I undertook to investigate their cause with a view of determining their length. As nothing can exist without a cause, synchronous and covariant phenomena regularly repeating themselves in cycles of uniform length, must have a permanent cause that is common to them all; and whatever that may be and wheresoever located, it must be ascertainable and susceptible of proof...

"In the preceding part of this work I have demonstrated that winds, rain, snow and hailstorms, cyclones, auroras, earthquakes, in fine, all telluric and atmospheric phenomena are electric; and that under what may be considered the normal condition of the Earth and the atmosphere the Electricity necessary to their production is constantly being generated but with varying energy...

"The testimony of the facts presented, incontestably establishes these points; that earthquakes have a periodicity in the frequency of their occurrence, and that they show well defined periods of maxims and minima, which alternate regularly as to time with each other. Examinations of the dates of their occurrences show that these maxima and minima are covariants with those of other physical disturbances...

"Earthquakes are caused by disruptive discharges of Electricity through the strata of the Earth. Electric currents, at all times, are circulating through the Earth from East to 'West. In times of physical perturbations, indicated by sunspots, auroras and great oscillations in the magnetic needle, earth currents, as they are called, often become too intense to be transmitted through the strata of the Earth, unless where the strata are unbroken or of good conductive capacity. These currents where the strata are broken up, or of too feeble conductive capacity, become damned up, as it were, until they are strong enough to force a passage, which is effected by what is called a disruptive discharge."

Copyright © 2020 by FV Éditions
Ebook ISBN : 979-10-299-0990-0
Paperback ISBN : 979-10-299-0991-7
Hardcover ISBN : 979-10-299-0992-4
All rights reserved.

www.ingramcontent.com/pod-product-compliance
Lightning Source LLC
LaVergne TN
LVHW092050060526
838201LV00047B/1327